WAGNER

The Terrible Man and His Truthful Art

The 1998 Larkin-Stuart Lectures

M. OWEN LEE

UNIVERSITY OF TORONTO PRESS
Toronto Buffalo London

© University of Toronto Press Incorporated 1999
Toronto Buffalo London
Printed in Canada

Reprinted 1999

ISBN 0-8020-4721-1 (cloth)
ISBN 0-8020-8291-2 (paper)

∞

Printed on acid-free paper

Canadian Cataloguing in Publication Data

Lee, M. Owen, 1930–
Wagner : the terrible man and his truthful art

'The 1998 Larkin-Stuart lectures.'
Includes bibliographical references and index.
ISBN 0-8020-4721-1 (bound)
ISBN 0-8020-8291-2 (pbk.)

1. Wagner, Richard, 1813–1883 – Criticism and interpretation. I. Title.

ML410.W13L47 1999   782.1'092   C99-930974-9

Portions of chapter 3 are reproduced from *First Intermissions* by
M. Owen Lee. Copyright © 1995 by Oxford University Press, Inc.
Used by permission of Oxford University Press, Inc.

University of Toronto Press acknowledges the financial assistance to
its publishing program of the Canada Council for the Arts and the
Ontario Arts Council.

We acknowledge the financial support of the Government of
Canada through the Book Publishing Industry Development
Program (BPIDP) for our publishing activities.

Canadä

WAGNER
The Terrible Man and His Truthful Art

M. Owen Lee

(The 1998 Larkin-Stuart Lectures)

How is it possible for a seriously flawed human being to produce art that is good, true, and beautiful? Why is the art of Richard Wagner, a very imperfect man, important and even indispensable to us?

In this volume, Father Owen Lee ventures an answer to those questions by way of a figure in Sophocles – the hero Philoctetes. Gifted by his god with a bow that would always shoot true to the mark and indispensable to his fellow Greeks, he was visited by the same god with an odious wound that made him hateful and hated. Sophocles' powerful insight is that those gifted by the gods and indispensable to men are visited as well with great vulnerability and suffering.

Wagner: The Terrible Man and His Truthful Art traces some of Wagner's extraordinary influence for good and ill on a century of art and politics – on Eliot and Proust as well as on Adolf Hitler – and discusses in detail Wagner's *Tannhäuser*, the work in which the composer first dramatised the Faustian struggle of a creative artist in whom 'two souls dwell.' In the course of this penetrating study, Father Lee argues that Wagner's ambivalent art is indispensable to us, life-enhancing and ultimately healing.

FATHER M. OWEN LEE, CSB, is a Catholic priest and Professor Emeritus of Classics at St Michael's College, University of Toronto, where he has recently received the Outstanding Teacher Award. For many years he has been internationally known as an intermission commentator, quizmaster, and panellist on the Metropolitan Opera radio broadcasts. Among his many books are *Wagner's Ring: Turning the Sky Round* (1991), *First Intermissions* (1995), *The Olive-Tree Bed and Other Quests* (1997), and *A Season of Opera: From Orpheus to Ariadne* (1998).

for
JON VICKERS
who in his art
deepened our awareness
of the things that matter

CONTENTS

PREFACE

I would like to thank Provost W. Thomas Delworth of Trinity College, University of Toronto, for inviting me to give the 1998 Larkin-Stuart lectures and for helping me to determine what my contribution to this distinguished series would be concerned with – not, as this classicist first suggested, Horace and his *Odes*, but the nineteenth-century composer whose life and work have been thought, throughout the twentieth century, to be controversial from many moral and ethical points of view – and so more germane than the genial Horace to the concerns of this lecture series.

I'd like also to thank former provost Robert Painter for introducing me on the first night with extremely generous words; Sue Polanyi, John Lawson, and Fathers Roy Hoult and Brian Freeland of St Thomas's Church for hospitality graciously, not to say joyously, given on the three memorable days; the great Canadian tenor Jon Vickers, who to my astonishment attended all three lectures with his wife, Judith; Professor William Blissett, who sent me copies of his perceptive articles on Wagner in the course of the writing and offered helpful criticism in preparing its revision; and Suzanne Rancourt, Barbara Porter, Kristen Pederson, and John St James for seeing the typescript into print.

This volume preserves the lectures substantially as

they were given on September 22, 23, and 24, 1998, from
the stage of the MacMillan Theatre in the Edward
Johnson Building on the campus of the University of Toronto.

M. Owen Lee
St Michael's College
University of Toronto
September 1998

CHAPTER ONE

Wagner and the Wound That Would Not Heal

These three Larkin-Stuart lectures, part of a series devoted to religious and ethical concerns, will examine some aspects of the life and work of Richard Wagner. This may be cause for some surprise, for Wagner was not a religious man in any conventional sense, nor could he be considered to have observed, in his life, particularly high ethical standards. In fact, his life, his works, and his influence have been, for more than a century, matters of controversy.[1] I have spoken and written over the years on many men and some women who have laboured in varied fields of artistic endeavour, and most of the time my remarks have been well received. Wagner, however, always prompts extreme reactions – rapturous responses from some and blistering missives, faxes, and phone calls from others. The mere mention of Wagner's name seems to call out both the uncritical worshippers and the fanatical debunkers, not to mention the axe-grinders, the militarists, the self-righteous, the non-normal. I often have to try to convince one camp that Wagner's very real faults and, in the first half of this century, baleful influence must be acknowledged. And I have to persuade the opposition that Wagner's ambivalent art is for many people – and they are not unfeeling or unintelligent – life-affirming and even indispensable.[2]

I have chosen Wagner for my subject here because, invited by Provost Delworth to consider both morality and music, Wagner seemed the figure in music whose work most poses a question related to this lecture series: how is it that a man some regard as morally corrupt could produce works of art that are, to many people of good conscience, indispensable?[3] Can a terrible man produce art that is good, true, and beautiful?

Before I address that question, let me say that my education some fifty years ago here at the University of Toronto had nothing to do with either Wagner or with Christian ethics. It was an education exclusively in the Classics of Greece and Rome, and much of my instruction, on both the undergraduate and graduate levels, I received at the institution under whose aegis these lectures are given annually – Trinity College. I read Greek drama with S.M. Adams, who seemed to us then so impossibly old, and spoke with such authority on the matter of how Sophocles was staged in antiquity, that we students were agreed that he *had* to have been in attendance at the Athens premieres in the fifth century BC. I read Latin verse at Trinity with E.A. Dale, a practical man of the theatre who, during the half-way break in his seminars, used to descend to the Buttery, which then was on the bottom floor of the old building, and shoo us histrionically from our coffee cups back upstairs to the perusal of Propertius. And I read Greek literary criticism and philosophy with one of Trinity's great classicists, George Maximilian Antony Grube, whose book on Plato's thought might have been written today, so strikingly modern and persuasive are the insights he drew from the philosopher of more than two thousand years past.

So, blessed by Trinity College as I have been, why should I not begin these lectures by telling a story, a Greek myth that all three of my Trinity professors touched on in their classes? It is the story of, as Edmund

Wilson once put it, a wound 'that lasts forever and a weapon that cannot fail.'[4] Wagner was widely read in the Greek Classics (in the famous German translations by Johann Gustav Droyson) and he knew very well the story I shall tell.[5] In fact, he put some of its elements into his syncretic, symbolic final musical statement, *Parsifal*. Elements of the story also crop up in his other work, for elements of it figured in his life.

The story tells how Apollo, god of music, once gave that most heroic of figures from Greek myth, Heracles, a bow that would unfailingly shoot an arrow straight to its mark. The mighty Heracles, armed with the god's bow, cleared a path in the world for the progress of civilization. And when his labours were done and the time came for him to die – to be immolated in his last agony in a great mountain-top conflagration, and so ascend to Olympus to become a god himself – the only comrade of his who could be persuaded to light the fatal fire was his devoted follower Philoctetes. In gratitude the dying Heracles bequeathed to Philoctetes the wondrous, unerring bow he had received from Apollo.

Philoctetes loved his new possession. That is what his name (philo-ktetes) means. It was with that beloved possession, that god-given bow, that Philoctetes set off to win glory with his fellow Greeks at the Trojan War. It was with that bow of Apollo that, en route to Troy, he led the way to Apollo's shrine at Chryse to sacrifice there. And (as we interpret the sources) it was at the shrine of the god whose wondrous bow he bore that Philoctetes was suddenly bitten in the foot by the tutelary serpent of Apollo's sacred place.

The wound began to fester and suppurate. It was impossible to perform the sacrifice. Philoctetes' comrades carried him aboard ship and journeyed on towards Troy. But his cries of pain were so excruciating, and the stench of his wound so unbearable, that, encouraged by their commanders, they finally abandoned Philoctetes, with his bow, on the island of Lemnos. Then they sailed on, deaf to the curses he sent after them.

The festering wound of Philoctetes would not heal. Neither would his obsessive hatred for those who had, he thought, betrayed him.

Meanwhile, at Troy, the Greeks found the city impregnable, cliffed and fortified on all sides by massive walls. (Let me say parenthetically that visiting the site of ancient Troy, standing alone on the Roman wall there, and looking down across the plain to the sea, was a moment in which I searched my soul, for the *Iliad* is my favourite book.) Homer tells how for nine long years the Greeks fought the Trojan armies on that windy plain between the city and the sea. Their casualties were great. In the tenth year they lost their best warrior, Achilles. Then they heard a prophecy that the city would never be taken unless the wounded Philoctetes was brought to Troy with his bow. So, after nine long years, they sent a ship back to the island of Lemnos to find him.

This is where a surviving play by Sophocles takes up the story. The *Philoctetes* of Sophocles, which I read at Trinity College in a graduate course with Professor Adams, is a play that, in the nineteen sixties, suddenly had an immense appeal to thousands of students in my country, the United States, because it seemed to address with uncommon accuracy certain issues, not of the Trojan, but of the Vietnam War. For Sophocles introduces at this point in the story an idealistic young soldier – Neoptolemus, whose name means 'new to the war.' Hardly more than a boy, Neoptolemus is the son of Achilles, eager to fight for his country and win glory as his father had done. But in the play he is made to be the Greeks' pawn in tricking Philoctetes to come to their aid with his indispensable bow.

The Greek ship puts in at rocky Lemnos, with the cunning Odysseus as its captain. Young Neoptolemus is told that he must first win the confidence of the wounded Philoctetes, and then lie to him. He must tell him that the ship has come to take him home. That is the only way they will get him and his all-important bow to come to Troy and win the war.

The youth is shocked and confused. But he follows orders: when he finds the wounded Philoctetes with his bow, in a cave high above the sea, tormented by pain and obsessed with hatred, he lies to him. He says he has come in pity to take him back to Greece. Philoctetes' implacable hatred begins to give way. We can see that, beneath the hate, he is a human being.

Then the wound breaks out afresh, and Philoctetes falls writhing to the ground. His pain is so great that he asks the youth to cut off his poisoned foot. The youth will not do that, and, when the spasms are past, he decides, out of a sense of honour, to disobey the orders of his superior officers, and keep his promise to take the sufferer home.

The other Greeks, in scenes that, in the manner of

Greek tragedy, break suddenly from speech into song, turn on their young recruit. The limping Philoctetes, cursing those who once abandoned him and now find they cannot do without him, threatens to throw himself off the cliff rather than sail with them, and he aims an arrow straight at the devious Odysseus.

The situation is solved only by the intervention of the one who first gave Philoctetes his indispensable bow: Heracles appears in the fullness of his godhead to tell the wounded, hateful man that his hatred is self-defeating, that his suffering has had a purpose, that if he goes with his fellow Greeks to Troy, he will be cured of his wound and win imperishable glory with the bow that all of them need. Heracles may be a *deus ex machina*, but he speaks to Philoctetes not as a god but as someone who has known suffering too. And in the end Philoctetes, of his own free will, sails for Troy to help those who need him.

I think you can see why this play appealed so strongly to young men disillusioned by the war in Vietnam. The Sophocles who wrote it knew the glory of war: when he himself was a youth, he was chosen to lead the victory procession through the streets of Athens after his Greeks had defeated the invading Persians. He also knew, from the subsequent war that his city waged with Sparta through the rest of his lifetime, about the claims of expediency in wartime, the compromises, the opportunism, the duplicity that can run unchecked in a military chain of command. But there is more than that in this story. Something important to our purpose here.

Sophocles was eighty-seven when he wrote the *Philoctetes*, and he followed it with another play I once read at Trinity College, a play about another specially gifted man, a man who saw more deeply into life than any of his contemporaries, who was wounded, and who wandered for years cursed by and cursing those who had abandoned him. Limping, self-blinded, contemptuous of others and utterly despised by them, this perceptive man too is suddenly found indispensable to, and is sought out by, those who had hated him – for an oracle has revealed that the place where he, Oedipus, will die will enjoy everlasting peace. *Oedipus at Colonus* was Sophocles' last play, a final statement made when he was ninety years old.

Behind both plays is the powerful insight of an artist at the end of his life – the perception that great gifts are given by the gods only at the price of great suffering and vulnerability. Great gifts leave the recipient wounded, isolated, unfulfilled: Philoctetes tells young Neoptolemus that he found his sole companions in his faithful bow, in the sound of the sea upon the rocks, and above all in his pain. 'That, my son, I meet at every turn.'

Both Sophoclean plays assert too that divinely bestowed gifts, and the incomprehensible burdens they impose, can provoke the contempt of one's fellow men, and prompt the gifted man to express *his* contempt, savagely, in reprisal. The rest of humanity is slow to realize its debt to the hateful, wounded man they are in need of. It might seem surprising to find Sophocles dramatizing this theme in his old age, for he was extraordinarily handsome, eminently successful, and honoured all his life. But he had his inner demons: they surface in all seven of his surviving plays, and he is said to have declared in his old age that he was happy to be released at last from one of them – erotic desire, which he called, if not quite a wound, at least a cruel and irrational master. The myth of Philoctetes was dramatized in fifth-century BC. Athens by Aeschylus and Euripides as well, but we know their versions only from prose summaries. Aeschylus seems to have made the story more heroic, and Euripides to have made it more squalid. Sophocles chose, as we might expect from his other plays, to give us a character study: through the eyes of an idealistic youth suddenly confronted with realities he has never suspected, we see an older man divinely gifted and at the same time divinely wounded, grown obsessively hateful, loathsome even to those who need him. Sophocles knew that the myth, susceptible of many meanings, was unusually perceptive about those endowed by divine dispensation with unerring insight.

Subsequent history has borne him out, at least when it comes to artists: our Beethovens, Michelangelos, and Dostoevskys, whom we need, whose art nurtures us and may even be indispensable to some of us, were not happy or well-adjusted men. That most erratic of poets, Byron, with his limping club foot, was never really accepted by his fellow countrymen, and remained proud and arrogant all his life – a master of invective, a lonely outcast from his own land who found redemption of sorts on the isles of Greece. He is the very image of the Romantic artist, creative but maimed.

But then the Greek god of creative artistry himself, Hephaestus, was, you will remember, lame – powerful in the shoulders and arms that did his wonderful creative

work, but limping on pitifully thin legs, an object of deri-
sion in the gatherings of the gods, the very image of the
artist of every age, creative but maimed.

Twenty-four centuries after Sophocles, another man,
psychologically wounded and at odds with society,
André Gide, wrote a new *Philoctetes* in which the suffering hero is, like himself, a writer. Gide's solitary artist
tells the young soldier who wants to take him from his
island that his suffering there has taught him more of the
secrets of life than he could possibly have learned had he
been a normal man functioning in and accepted by society. Edmund Wilson, in his study *The Wound and the Bow*,
notes that the Philoctetes of Gide is 'an artist whose
genius becomes purer and deeper in ratio to his isolation
and outlawry.'[6]

Outlawry. I guess that brings us back to Wagner, for
the manic little man with the outsized head, when he
turned thirty-six, had to flee his Germany with a price on
that head for his participation in the Dresden uprising of
1849. (Some of his fellow revolutionaries were con-
demned to death, though the sentences were eventually
commuted to long prison terms.) Wagner languished in
exile for twelve years, sketching through some of that
time an opera he never completed – on a figure from
German mythology, Wieland the Smith, a marvellous
artisan who is lame, held in bondage, and finally escapes
on wings of his own devising. Wagner, by all accounts a
monstrously flawed man, given to venting his spleen
indiscriminately in all directions, was also greatly gifted
and – this isn't said often enough – a tormented man,
vulnerable and suffering. The most famous single essay

on him, by Thomas Mann, got it right. It is titled, in the
translation by H.T. Lowe-Porter, not 'The Greatness' but
'The *Sufferings* and Greatness of Richard Wagner.'

So I want, on this first of our three evenings, to state
the Wagner case by way of Philoctetes. However defec-
tive Wagner may have been as a man, however detest-
able his obsessive ranting, we need his unerring art. It is
as necessary to us as was the bow of Philoctetes to his fellow Greeks, whether we are sympathetic, like young
Neoptolemus, or unsympathetic, like Odysseus. (In the
next lecture I shall comment on the influence of Wagner
for good and ill on this century now hurrying to its end.
And my final lecture will be devoted entirely to one of
Wagner's operas, partially to support my observations.
But first it shall be Wagner as Philoctetes, hateful and yet
indispensable.)

Was Wagner a hateful man? There is plenty of evidence
that he was. Now that we have his own journal, the
Brown Book, and the diaries of his second wife, Cosima,
the daughter of Franz Liszt, to add to Wagner's own
autobiography and voluminous correspondence, newly
edited, we may know more about him than we know
about any man in history till the advent of the tape
recorder. But we are only with difficulty beginning to get
the facts straight, and the interpretation of the facts is
still controversial. For two decades now it has been said
that more has been written about Wagner than about any
other person who ever lived except Jesus and, just possibly, Napoleon. That may or may not be true.[7] But controversy is what gets ink spilled. And controversy is what

has always surrounded the lives and the ambivalent legacies of the French conqueror who almost destroyed Europe and the German maker of myths in music about whom, in some quarters, the same is said.

All ten of Wagner's mature operas (the devout call them music dramas) still hold the stages of the world's opera houses – *The Flying Dutchman, Tannhäuser, Lohengrin,* the four parts of the massive cycle *Der Ring des Nibelungen,* that erotic masterpiece *Tristan und Isolde,* my own favourite *Die Meistersinger,* and the final *Parsifal.*

Earlier, Wagner tested himself, operatically speaking, in older German traditions (with *Die Feen*), in Italian traditions (with *Das Liebesverbot*), and, in an all-out bid for international popular success, in the French traditions of the five-act grand opera (with *Rienzi*). I won't be talking about those early works, which Wagner later referred to as the sins of his youth.

And we can be relatively brief about his other sins, for they are well known and well documented: yes, the long-exiled Wagner was an utterly self-absorbed artist who lied, cheated, and betrayed friend and foe alike; who did not scruple to use people for his own ends; who despised conventional morality and had no patience with those who disagreed with him; who acknowledged no equals to his own genius, with the possible exceptions of the classic Greeks, Shakespeare, and a few Germans, notably Beethoven – all of whose achievements he claimed to be lifting to greater heights; whose often dubious ideas were published in sometimes appallingly vicious pamphlets; whose contradictory nature is perhaps best illustrated by his luxuriating in silken garments amid attar of roses in a damasked room while he composed dramas about self-denial and renunciation; who had stormy love affairs with many women, most of them married;[8] whose first wife reached a point where she found it impossible to put up with his infidelities; whose second wife he impregnated three times before he stole her away from a man who was utterly devoted to him and had sacrificed years of his life for him.

Today there is an almost comic aspect to Wagner's egotism, self-absorption, and success in dominating those he wanted to use. I recall Victor Borge describing a typical case: Wagner always wrote his own libretti, usually long before he set them to music, and he used to call in groups of friends to listen patiently as he read through his latest text. The friends dutifully came, with the knowledge that they were there, not to criticize, but to approve: they were expected to like what they heard, and to say so. Well, when Wagner completed the text of that famous music drama about adulterous and uncontrollable passion, *Tristan und Isolde*, he read it aloud to his wife, his mistress, his mistress's husband, his future mistress, and his future mistress's husband. And they all said they liked it.

When I was a boy, a young Neoptolemus new to Wagner controversies, everyone seemed to know and to quote from a witty essay by Deems Taylor called 'Wagner the Monster.' Indignant people still send me copies of it in the mail after I've said something nice about Wagner on the Met broadcasts. Taylor, after detailing instances of Wagner's 'delusions of grandeur,' his 'mania for being in the right,' his emotional instability (raving and stamping if things went wrong, running out and climbing a tree or standing on his head if things went right, 'grief-stricken over the death of a pet dog' but with people 'callous and heartless to a degree that would have made a Roman emperor shudder'), thinking not just that he was 'the most important person in the world but that he was the only person who ever existed', that 'he was Shakespeare, and Beethoven, and Plato rolled into one' – after all that and more, Taylor says, 'The curious thing about this record is that ... this undersized, sickly, disagreeable, fascinating little man was right all along ... He *was* one of the world's great dramatists; he *was* a great thinker; he *was* one of the most stupendous musical geniuses that, up to now, the world has ever seen. The world did owe him a living.'[9]

There is some overstatement there: Wagner was widely read in literature of all sorts, and his head was seething with ideas all his life – he invariably needed the stimulus of ideas in order to create – but I don't think Taylor is justified in calling him 'a great thinker.' For one thing, most of the ideas that inspired his creations he discarded once the creation was done. And Taylor doesn't mention how bilious some of those ideas were. He doesn't mention Wagner's very real and almost pathological anti-Semitism. Taylor wrote his amusing piece on Wagner before any of us knew what was to happen to six million Jews in the Second World War – a horror Wagner has, increasingly in recent years, been held partly responsible for, and something I hope I may postpone discussion of until the second of these lectures. But Taylor does acknowledge what few have acknowledged in

the matter of Wagner – the vulnerability that turned him
into a ranting Philoctetes. The rejection. The pain. 'That,
my son, I meet at every turn.'
All of Wagner's heroes are, in today's parlance, mar-
ginalized, as Philoctetes was. Siegmund, in many ways
the most sympathetic of them, says, 'Misfortune has
always followed me. Everywhere I am rejected. And so it
was wherever I went.' Wagner, like many creative artists
but to an extreme degree, could not rest, for he was com-
pelled – he sometimes said he was sentenced – by some
inner demon to write the immense body of work he had
outlined for himself one summer when he was only
thirty-two: he had to dramatize for his Germans what
Germany meant – from the Grail myths to the heroic
saga of Siegfried to the historic splendours of German
lyric art – just as, when drama was born, the classic
Greek playwrights had dramatized for *their* people *their*
mythic heritage, and so shown them themselves, and
created a great civilization. It was for this daunting purpose that Wagner did not scruple to pre-empt to himself
more than other men of genius presumed to. And he suffered in the process. The once-traditional picture of Wagner as the confident egotist self-indulgently composing
at his ease is almost completely false. To read his letters
and the diaries of his wife Cosima is to read a day-by-
day account of a man plagued with self-doubt, self-pity,
and self-destructive impulses, in flight and frustration
and fear, recurrently in the grip of erysipelas or Roem-
held's Syndrome or, near the end, increasingly frequent
heart spasms, ever in need of support, often emotionally
isolated, grasping at the ideas of others – some of them

admirable, some of them deplorable – and then desper-
ately trying to convince himself that they were *his* ideas;
issuing statements on every conceiveable subject and yet
agonized because he could not understand himself. The
long duologues in the *Ring* between Wotan and Fricka,
between Wotan and Brünnhilde, between Wotan and
Erda (passages that casual opera-goers find so uninter-
esting) are quite patently Wagner questioning himself,
debating with, respectively, his conscience, his will, and
his intuition – all of them, interestingly, embodied in
female figures. Wagner was 'seeking self-understanding'[10] in those monumental scenes, so like the duologues
in Greek tragedy, though when self-understanding
comes at the end of his dramas, it comes not in words or
arguments but in symbols and orchestral perorations.

Meanwhile, in much of his day-to-day life, Wagner
was a ranting Philoctetes. When he was provoked he
'would roar like a tiger. He paced the room like a caged
lion... the words came like screams; his speech slashed
about at random. He seemed at these times like some ele-
mental force unchained.' (That is the report of Édouard
Schuré, a playwright and critic who knew Wagner, and
knew him well, during his *Tristan* period.)[11]

One fairly obvious way to account for the artistic wonders wrought by this neurotically driven man is via
Alfred Adler's compensatory theory of creativity as outlined by the psychologist Rollo May: 'Human beings
produce art, science, and other aspects of culture to com-
pensate for their own inadequacies. The oyster produc-
ing the pearl to cover up the grain of sand intruding into
its shell is often cited as a simple illustration.'[12]

But Dr May does not accept this reductive theory completely, and neither do I, because it centres on the artist's neurosis and never accounts for the greatness of his art. The wise Greek myth puts it more tellingly: the artist cannot wield the bow given by the god without suffering from the wound given by the god. He cannot create without suffering.[13] 'The self-destructive element in Wagner' is, as Robert Donington put it, 'the negative aspect of his vast creative activity.'[14] But it is the art that the vast creative activity produces that matters.

Wagner wrote an opera – his greatest, I think – on the subject of the artist's creativity. Without this opera, *Die Meistersinger*, we would be at a loss to account for some of the things, so unlike our Philoctetes-image, that we read of in Cosima's diaries: Wagner's often sunny disposition, his sometimes overwhelming charm, his astonishingly wide reading interests, his endless curiosity about everything in life. In the second act of *Die Meistersinger*, he has his Hans Sachs, a good, wise, learned, and compassionate man, wonder how someone so hot-headed, callow, and foolish as young Walther von Stolzing could create a song that is a marvel of beauty. As Sachs wonders, Wagner's music, synaesthetically aglow with the scent of the leaves of an elder tree on a moonlit night, gets us memorably inside the cobbler-poet's head: Sachs concludes, metaphorically (for everything in *Die Meistersinger* is metaphorical), 'A songbird sings because he must, and because he must he can.' That is to say, a true artist creates in response to an overwhelming inner compulsion, a 'süsse Not,' which demands that he exceed his own limitations, and actually *enables* him to do so. Wag-

ner created because he had to – paradoxically, out of the
abundance of his own need. In Wagner's case, it was the
only way: what he could not achieve in his life he had to
and ultimately did achieve in his work – integrity, greatness of soul, human understanding.

Donington remarks that, in another soliloquy in *Die
Meistersinger*, Hans Sachs, pouring over his book of history, 'reflects sadly on the mad streak, the manic streak,
that runs through human nature like some tragic flaw in
bright metal,' and then resolves to use this potentially
destructive flaw for constructive ends. For it is out of the
flaw in human nature (out of the potential in man for
good and evil that Wagner calls *Wahn* and Christians call
the consequences of original sin) that great works of art
come. Or so Hans Sachs, on the feast day of John the Bap-
tist, tells young Walther in another one of Wagner's long
and insightful duologues. Donington concludes, I think
rightly, 'The neurotic drive and the creative drive are not
different forces but the same force at its negative and
positive poles.'[15] In short, the wound and the bow are
complementary elements in the gift given by the god of
music.

I don't doubt that great art can be produced by a good
man. (Bach comes immediately to mind.) But in most
cases great art is produced by someone deeply divided,
profoundly ambivalent, ever-conscious of the flaw in
human nature, struggling with it, and endowed by it
with a potential for good or ill much vaster than our
own. That, to a considerable extent, is what makes their
art worth having. That is why the central image in *Die
Meistersigner* is baptism, the sacrament which cleanses

the soul of original sin. But all of Wagner's works, and especially the mature works, are about the healing of the hurt in, the drawing off of the evil in, the integration of the conflicting forces in, the human psyche.

The unconvinced, hearing this said about a hateful, ranting man, will point out that the very solutions Wagner called for in humankind at large he was unable to find in himself. But that, as Hans Sachs sings in *Die Meistersinger*, is why the artist creates. Wagner, like the Philoctetes of Sophocles, needed healing and wholeness. His operas massively strive for, and in the end achieve, the completeness we all hope to find in the lives given us to lead. Ultimately the self-absorbed Wagner wrote for the rest of us.

We've spoken much about the wound in Wagner's nature. What of the god-given bow, that is to say, Wagner's art? Is it, as Apollo's bow was, indispensable for the rest of us? As necessary to us as that bow was to the Greeks at the Trojan War? I would say that it is, if not altogether necessary, at the very least salutary. It can be salutary, first, to society as a whole, if we can read it rightly. In his mature works Wagner 'said what few others in his seemingly progressive century were saying – that the West was actually in decline, due partly to its technology and its dehumanizing industrialization, partly to its loss of spiritual values.'[16] In the *Ring* Wagner tells us that we are headed for world destruction if we cannot develop a political system that does not use money for power. In *Parsifal* he tells us we will not survive if we cannot devise an ethical system that recognizes and contravenes our self-destructive urges. In *Die Meistersinger* he tells his Germans that it is not mindless adherence to the past, not arrogance or pride of noble birth, and certainly not military might, that they should look to for their future. They should value above all art that looks deeply into the soul and offers understanding. If Germany failed to see the import of this in the first half of the twentieth century, when *Die Meistersinger* was made an emblem of Nazism, Germany recognized that failure in the last half of the century, as it turned from militarism to the arts of peace and its half-hundred opera houses reopened – with dedicatory performances of *Die Meistersinger*.

But is Wagner's art salutary to individual people? Can it help *you* to see into your problems, and me into mine? The most insightful commentators on Wagner, and certainly the most famously ambivalent, are Friedrich Nietzsche and Thomas Mann. When Nietzsche first heard the prelude to *Parsifal*, he wrote, overawed, 'It was as if someone were speaking to me again, after many years, about the problems that disturb me.'[17] Apropos of *Tristan* he said, with characteristic irony, 'All things considered, I could not have endured my youth without Wagner's music ... I think I know better than anyone else of what tremendous things Wagner is capable – the fifty worlds of alien ecstasies for which no one besides him had wings; and given the way I am, strong enough to turn even what is most questionable and dangerous to my advantage and thus to become stronger, I call Wagner the great benefactor of my life.'[18]

'Even what is most questionable and dangerous': Thomas Mann, like Nietzsche fully aware of the dangers of an uncritical approach to Wagner, wrote that his passion for the composer's art was a part of his life ever since he first became aware of it: 'All that I owe to him, of enjoyment and instruction, I can never forget: the hours of deep and single bliss in the midst of the theatre crowds, hours of nervous and intellectual transport and rapture, of insights of great and moving import such as only this art vouchsafes.'[19]

More recently Bernard Levin said in the London *Times*: 'No other composer goes down into such dark and forbidden chasms ... nor up to such blinding brightnesses ... Wagner is dangerous. He liberates passions high and low, he breaks open doors that we try all our lives to shut, he tears bandages off ancient, unhealing wounds. Go to Wagner's *Ring* and at the end of the week you have had the equivalent of a year in the psychiatrist's chair. Go to *Tristan und Isolde* thrice and you are lucky to be alive.' 'I am a true Wagnerite,' he continues, speaking for many of us, 'and I have long ago surrendered my subconscious to him.' Speaking for me, Levin says he has noticed that 'there are more clergymen in an opera house on Wagner nights than when other composers are on the bill ... I do not find that strange,' he says. 'Priests, too, have passions to wrestle with.'[20] The Catholic theologian Hamish Swanston, particularly eloquent on those long duologues in the *Ring*, says simply, 'To appreciate [Wagner's] music is to enlarge one's understanding of oneself.'[21]

The famous artists who have expressed personal indebtedness to Wagner are legion, and almost always they admit that they have found themselves, understood themselves, in the music. Baudelaire, to quote only one of them, said when he first heard the preludes to *Tannhäuser* and *Lohengrin*, 'What I felt was indescribable ... I felt I already knew this music. It seemed to me that this was my music.' He spoke of floating in an ecstasy compounded of joy and insight, and wrote to Wagner to say, 'Thank you ... You have brought me back in touch with myself.'[22]

But of course Baudelaire's was a profoundly ambivalent self. There is no question that with Wagner we are coming closer than many of us would like to what is repressed and potentially threatening in ourselves. 'Wagner is dangerous stuff,' said Britain's leading conductor, Sir Colin Davis, in an interview for the *New York Times*. 'It is better to be in some possession of your faculties before you get involved in it.' About *Tristan* he said (and the *Times* reporter noted that at this point he lowered his voice almost to a whisper), 'The first contact with the thing is so overwhelming ... The third act, especially ... When you're conducting it, it's touch and go. You're just holding on.'[23] Sir Colin told me once in London that, while he had finally come to terms with Wagner's other works, he still could not understand or come to terms with the final *Parsifal*, and to this day he has not touched it. Not to conduct Wagner, he has said, would be impoverishing. But to do so requires a strong rudder and a dependable compass.

The fact is that Wagner's dramas plunge us through myth and music deep into ourselves, and what we discover there – often primitive, frightening, vindictive, and erotic – are the feelings that we who have constructive roles in society have suppressed. We may have relegated those desires beneath the level of consciousness, but none of us has completely tamed them. Many of those who detest Wagner do so because they realize that his music reaches that subconscious level as no other music does.[24] Wagner knew he was doing this. That is why he gave such prominence, in his operas, to the orchestra. 'There,' he said, 'the primal urges of creation and nature are represented. What the orchestra expresses can never be clearly articulated, because it renders primal feeling itself.' 'The vocal line,' he continued, 'is different from this. It represents ... human emotions that are intelligible and individuated.' No wonder that when we are first exposed to Wagner our attention goes to the orchestra. It seems to put us in touch with the very depths of our unconscious feelings.

And through that music, on Wagner's stage, we meet the very archetypes our century has discovered in the human psyche. The wounded Amfortas, the ambivalent Kundry, the wise old Gurnemanz, the Grail restored by Parsifal to wholeness and holiness – these are Carl Jung's archetypes of, respectively, the shadow, the anima, the Wise Old Man, and the Self. Wagner's final work, *Parsifal*, is of all his works the one most clearly about the healing of the hurt in, the drawing off of the evil in, the integration of the conflicting forces in, the human psyche. But *all* of the mature works are in the last analysis concerned with the healing of the wound, the draining away of evil and the bringing together of good, within us. That is something each of us needs. And Wagner's art, more than any other I know, is where we can find it.

I don't doubt that one can find similar release on his knees in church, or at the psychiatrist's, or especially in doing good work to help others in need. But Wagner's art is not unrelated to those other healing experiences. The English philosopher Bryan Magee contends that in Wagner's music 'some people are made to feel ... that they are in touch with the depths of their personalities for the first time. The feeling is of a wholeness yet unboundedness – hence ... its frequent comparison with mystical or religious experience.'[25] For many of us who know Wagner, the four great works – the *Ring*, *Tristan*, *Die Meistersinger*, and *Parsifal* – are a succession of related truths that make sense of the world.[26]

So even the genial Deems Taylor could say, at the end of his amusing piece, 'What if [Wagner] was faithless to his friends and to his wives? He had one mistress to whom he was faithful to the day of his death: Music. Not for a single moment did he ever compromise with what he believed, with what he dreamed. There is not a line of his music that could have been conceived by a little mind. Listening to his music, one does not forgive him for what he may or may not have been. It is not a matter of forgiveness. It is a matter of being dumb with wonder that his poor brain and body didn't burst under the torment of the demon of creative energy that lived inside him, struggling, clawing, scratching to be released; tearing, shrieking at him to write the music that was in him. The miracle is that what he did in the little space of seventy years could have been done at all, even by a great genius. Is it any wonder,' Taylor concludes, 'that he had no time to be a man?'[27]

One of the most impressive men I have ever met, at
once scholarly, saintly, and down-to-earth (I always
thought he looked like a bartender out of *Irma La Douce*),
was Étienne Gilson, the historian of philosophy who
taught for many years at my college – St Michael's – here
at the University of Toronto. Gilson never made his pilgrimage to Wagner's theatre at Bayreuth, though in his
last years he told me he dearly wanted to do so. And he
once wrote, apropos of Wagner, 'What would it mean if
[he] had kept for himself all he has generously poured
out in his works, if the substance so lavishly scattered
among his characters had been used in the creation of his
own character and personality?' Wagner himself wondered whether, if he had not given himself over wholly
to his art, he might have become a good man. He chose
instead to give us *Tristan* and *Die Meistersinger*. Gilson
remarks, I think rightly, 'An artist needs immense heroism to consent to this.'[28]

Let me conclude these preliminary remarks on Wagner
with the words in which Edmund Wilson sums up that
Greek play Wagner read and reread in admiration, the
Philoctetes. Wilson says about Sophocles' hate-filled hero
with the indispensable bow: 'The victim of a malodorous
disease which renders him abhorrent to society and peri-
odically degrades him and makes him helpless is also the
master of a superhuman art which everybody has to
respect and which the normal man finds he needs ... It is
in the nature of things – of this world where the divine
and the human fuse – that [one] cannot have the irresist-
ible weapon without its loathsome owner.'[29]

That's how Wilson put it. Let me put it slightly differently for our concerns here. Let me suggest that the god of music – call him Apollo if you will – gave Wagner, through the Herculean predecessor Wagner venerated, Ludwig von Beethoven,[30] a wonderful, powerful gift, and then visited on him characteristics many have thought loathsome, so that he hated and was hated. But because of his wounding this hateful man saw deeper into human depths, the good and the evil there, than any other composer ever had. And from his unerring insight, which aims straight at the sources of corruption within ourselves, we can, if we will, come to know and heal ourselves.

And that is why, if like young Neoptolemus we can see Wagner in all the ambivalence of his humanity, we should take him on our own personal journeys to the walls of Troy, to help us with our lives.

NOTES

1 The effect Wagner's work had on morals was not always thought harmful. Blissett 1959, 313–14 describes the 'Pauline' dedication of an English Wagnerite of Shaw's day, David Irvine, 'preaching of Wagner in season and out of season – Wagner as poet and thinker and moral teacher.' But already the Wagnerolatry had its dark side: Irvine thought that Wagner's obsequious blacksmith Mime, the sole instructor of young Siegfried, represented 'the craft which finds its best soil in the Church, impressing everyone in early youth, before judgement is ripe,' and that Siegfried forging his father's sword anew represented the free man who would destroy 'the alloy of egoistic, optimistic Judaism.' Blissett's valuable article details how such extremes were held at bay in England when the great Wagner scholar Ernest Newman 'applied the brakes' (322).

We could use some of Newman's good sense in braking today's
Wagnerian extremists.

2 W.H. Auden makes a telling distinction here: 'For the strong, the
intelligent, the healthy, the successful, those on whom, just
because they are so, falls the duty of understanding weakness,
stupidity, disease, and failure in order that they may cure them,
Wagner's operas are essential, a constant source of delight. They
must listen to him. But who should never be allowed to listen to
Wagner? The unhappy, the disappointed, the politically ambitious, the self-pitying, those who imagine themselves misunder-
stood, the Wagnerians.' Quoted in Rather 1990, v.

3 This is a question raised *mutatis mutandis* by recent biographies of
such varied figures as Albert Einstein and Niels Bohr (by Abra-
ham Pais), Ludwig Wittgenstein and Bertrand Russell (by Ray
Monk), Alan Turing (by Andrew Hodges), Thomas Jefferson (by
Joseph J. Ellis), James Joyce and T.S. Eliot (by several authors).
There is an increasingly prevalent tendency to see a man's important work in terms of his imperfect life. Cornwell 1997, 105 quotes
the neurologist Oliver Sachs on the symbiosis of the genius and
the disease: when Sachs had cured a brilliant mathematician of his
migraines, he admitted, 'The trouble was that I had cured him of
his mathematics as well. His abilities went into decline once his
headaches disappeared.'

4 Wilson 1941, 275.

5 See *Opera und Drama*, in Wagner 1911–16, 4: 64, and *Cosima Wagner's Diaries* 1977, entries for 24 May 1870, 11 and 12 April 1882,
and especially 16 April 1882 ('He agrees with me in my praise for
Philoctetes'). Wagner was immensely well read, with a collection of
some two thousand books in his library at Wahnfried, ranging
from Homer through Darwin and Carlyle – though he seems not
to have read such contemporaries as Dickens and Ibsen, and never
to have expressed an interest in Karl Marx.

6 Wilson 1941, 289.

7 Cf. Millington 1992, 132: 'There is no truth in the statement what-
soever, but no book about Wagner would be complete without it.
That more myths and legends have been propagated about Wag-

ner than about any other composer in the history of music might
be an easier proposition to sustain.'

8 William Blissett, in this connection, wrote to me privately, 'Wagner
in 1848 was an archetypal liberal-anarchist revolutionary. How
many of his contemporaries in art and ideology settled into stable
marriages? I can think of one – Karl Marx. This is the age of Franz
Liszt, of Napoleon III, of the Prince of Wales, afterward Edward
VII ... [And] compared with many twentieth-century writers, artists, and composers, Wagner's erotic affairs, if not his financial
dealings, verge on propriety. He cannot be called depraved or
debauched or a predator. He was a highly imaginative and (there-
fore?) highly concupiscent man.'

9 Taylor 1937, 363–6.

10 Swanston 1978, 202. That Swanston is factually wrong on a number of points and questionable in some of his interpretations does
not substantially diminish the value of his book, in particular the
remarkable pages on *Fidelio*, the *Ring*, *Otello*, *Pelléas et Mélisande*,
and *Ariadne auf Naxos*.

11 Reported by Peter Burbidge in Burbidge and Sutton, 1979, 17.

12 May 1975, 37.

13 Other psychological explanations of Wagner's creativity are Pus-
chmann, 1873 (Wagner was mentally ill); Nietzsche, 1888 (Wagner
was 'une névrose'); Nordau, 1895 (Wagner was suffering from
persecution mania, megalomania, graphomania [*sic*] and several
other disorders); Lombroso, 1897 (Wagner was a sexual psycho-
path); Fuchs, 1903, Panizza, 1895, and the unaptly named Pudor,
1907 (Wagner was a repressed homosexual); Graf, 1911, and Rank,
1911 (Wagner suffered from an Oedipus complex); Spielrein, 1912
(Wagner's sexual instinct led to a fixation on death); the aptly
named Swisher, 1923 (Wagner was fixated at the anal stage);
Wulffen, 1928 (Wagner had pathological criminal tendencies); and
Racker, 1948 (Wagner suffered from unresolved pregenital conflicts). All of these plus several Jungian studies (which examine
the work apart from the man) and some post-Freudian analyses of
Wagner's dreams (as recorded in Cosima's diaries) are discussed
by Isolde Vetter in Müller and Wapnewski 1992, 118–55, who con-

cludes (147) that 'whole armies of experts from a variety of psychological disciplines have fallen on Wagner without ultimately being able to discover anything sufficiently specific in his artistic persona that would "explain" his artistry or his art.'

14 Donington 1976, 18.
15 Donington 1976, 19.
16 Lee 1998, 201.
17 Quoted in Beckett 1979, 382.
18 Nietzsche, 'Ecce Homo,' 2.6.
19 Mann 1933, 324.
20 Levin, 'Music from the depths,' from the *London Times*, ca. 1993.
21 Swanston 1978, 57.
22 Letter of 17 February 1860. Quoted in Barth, Mack, and Voss 1975, 193.
23 From an interview with Joseph Horowitz, 'He has made peace with Romanticism,' *New York Times*, 10 December 1978.
24 For a similar statement on Wagner's giving expression to repressed but still powerful 'instinctual desires,' see Magee 1988 [1968], 34. The incest in *Die Walküre*, so romantically treated by Wagner and so detested by many intelligent people (Schopenhauer exclaimed, 'This is infamous!'), may be an instance of this. But more importantly, the incestuous love of Siegmund and Sieglinde is essential to Wagner's dramatic purposes in the *Ring*: it illustrates 'nature in conflict with law,' and points up the flaw in (and ultimately defeats) Wotan's initial plan to free the world from the laws he has imposed upon it. See Dalhhaus 1977 [1971], 89. (It should also be said that Wagner did not invent the incestuous situation in *Die Walküre*. It was an essential part of one of his sources, the Völsunga Saga.)
25 Magee 1988 [1968], 39.
26 This is the well-argued thesis of Tanner 1979, 140–224.
27 Taylor 1937, 366.
28 Gilson 1953, 192–3.
29 Wilson 1941, 294.
30 On Beethoven's heritage passing to Wagner cf. Magee 1988 [1968], 9–10: 'Beethoven, the first composer to proclaim his inner conflicts, had developed in music the power to articulate the inmost

drama of the psyche, but because his expressive means were confined to those of absolute music he could give utterance only to generalized emotions ... [until] in the last movement of his last symphony he introduced, for the first time, poetry. It was this combination of poetry and symphony that provided the take-off point for Wagner.' This observation overlooks *Fidelio* and some of the songs, but it is substantially correct.

CHAPTER TWO

Wagner's Influence: The First Hundred Years

W e shall be talking tonight about the pervasive influence, for good and ill, that Wagner has exercised through the hundred and more years since his death – an impingement on music, art, literature, politics, and psychology so vast that the philosopher Bryan Magee is able to say, 'Wagner has had a greater influence than any other single artist on the culture of our age.'[1]

That is a statement that is likely to seem exaggerated to anyone educated at this university, or at most North American institutions of higher learning. Until the international boom in Wagner studies that began in the nineteen sixties and seventies, Wagner was often scorned and dismissed, even hated and feared, in English-speaking academe. Two decades ago, the classicist Hugh Lloyd-Jones could find no study in English on Wagner's consuming interest in classic Greece save one dated and inadequate PhD thesis. One reason for the neglect of Wagner was of course his notorious life. The sins of his contemporaries – Baudelaire, Liszt, Tolstoy, Verlaine – we had long since made allowances for. But those artists seemed such ordinary sinners next to Wagner, and their art less suspect. And of course there is more to the matter than that. Since the Second World War Wagner more than any other man of genius has been held to task for his unquestioned influence on Adolf Hitler. On the other hand, new studies have begun seriously to investigate other influences – the influence, on Wagner, of Aeschylus and Sophocles, of Feuerbach and Schopenhauer, and the influence, of Wagner, on symbolist poets, impressionist painters, expressionist composers, and stream-of-consciousness novelists. We have begun to appreciate in

Wagner a startling anticipation of the psychological dis-
coveries of Freud and Jung, and of the modern structural
approach to myth. Our age has seen the unexpected
emergence, after decades of neglect, of the music of such
Wagner disciples as Bruckner and Mahler. We have
finally conceded that Wagner influenced, not just Richard Strauss, Schoenberg, and Berg, but Debussy in *Pelléas
et Mélisande*, Puccini in his middle period, and even
(though it was once *de rigeur* to deny this) the crowning
works of his great rival, Verdi. Wagner also originated
the idea of a festival long before our Stratfords and
Salzburgs. The stage techniques developed by his grand-
sons at Bayreuth – possibly the most revolutionary since
Wagner's own in the same theatre a century before –
have swept across Europe and America. Wagner is probably the single most important figure in the history of
orchestral conducting. It has been an altogether extraordinary influence.

Wagner might have been surprised by it all: when he
was writing his last opera, he said to his second wife,
Cosima, 'After my death I expect to be forgotten for a
hundred years.'[2] Presumably, then (that is to say, now)
the influence would really take hold. It has.

Let's begin our consideration of Wagner's influence
with another story[3] about *Tristan und Isolde*, which of all
his works has most affected music and the other arts.
Tristan is, as many of you will know, a tortuous work, a
long work, and one that makes almost unendurable
demands on both performers and listeners.

A friend of mine once went to see a performance of
Tristan at the old Metropolitan Opera House in New

York, on 39th Street and Broadway. He sat alone in a box at what was by all reports a superlative performance and, as he put it himself, he suffered the torments of the damned. He thought Act I ear-splitting and intolerably long. Act II was occasionally quieter, but seemed even longer. And through both acts, he felt like that martyr in a medieval painting often mentioned in connection with *Tristan* – the unfortunate whose innards are slowly and painfully being extracted on a wheel. When the curtain rose on Act III, and my friend saw the tenor, who had already agonized through most of a long evening, sprawled on the stage wounded and delirious, while a melancholy pipe wailed interminably in the orchestra, he knew that he was in for at least another hour of the same tortures, and he fled the theatre.

Not without some feelings of guilt, mind you. He was a professor of French literature at this university, and he knew all too well that, even in France where indigenous culture is part of the national pride, *Tristan* was one of the most influential of all works of art. That's why I chided him, on his return here from New York, for his inability to come to terms with *Tristan*: I told him a book had just come off the university presses, tracing the remarkable influence *Tristan* has had on art and thought through the twentieth century, and called *The First Hundred Years of Wagner's Tristan.*

'I knew it was long,' he said. 'But I didn't know it was *that* long!'

As I speak tonight on Wagner's influence, my first, unenviable, task – in this lecture series devoted to ethical concerns – is to address the issue of Wagner's influence for ill. The next fifteen minutes may not be easy to listen to. To be honest about this matter, however, it has got to be 'no holds barred.'

When, in 1945, the brassy glories of Wagner's *Siegfried* and *Götterdämmerung* were blended in popular imagination with the newsreel footage of Allied forces entering the concentration camps of Europe and standing aghast at the horrors, the end seemed plainly to have come for the arrogant Teuton whom Hitler had made his own and who, three-quarters of a century before, had appropriated art, politics, philosophy, and almost everything else in sight to fashion his gigantic *Gesamtkunstwerke*, his all-embracing operatic works of art, with the intent thereby of changing Germany if not the world. And yet the eclipse of Wagner, so confidently predicted through the decades that followed on the fall of the Nazis, has not taken place. For Wagner was not quite the monster our propaganda and his made him out to be.

I said earlier that he wrote not only gigantic music dramas but whole shelves of prose works on all manner of subjects. He probably wreaked more havoc on himself with his essay 'Judaism in Music' than with anything else he wrote. Published anonymously in 1850, and in a revised version under his own name in 1869, some time before the terms 'racist' and 'anti-Semitic' were coined, but of course following on centuries of widespread anti-Jewish feeling, of terrible pogroms and humiliating ghettoization, its central argument was that an artist must be true to his national traditions, and that a great artist must articulate in his work the needs, hopes, and ideals of his own country. That was an idea not, at first, much different from the expressed views of Verdi, Dvořák, and the Russian 'Group of Five.'[4] But Wagner went on to say that this nationalistic mission could not possibly be undertaken by a Jewish artist, given his rootlessness in the European countries into which the diaspora had sent him. 'Mendelssohn,' he said (he was seldom hesitant about naming names) 'has shown us that a Jew can have the richest abundance of specific talents, be a man of the broadest yet most refined culture, of the loftiest, most impeccable integrity, and yet not be able, not even with the help of all these qualities, to produce in us that deep, heart-seizing, soul-searching experience that we expect from art.'[5]

That, however deeply Wagner may have felt it, is not an admirable thesis. And it is no justification of it to say that it grew out of Wagner's own experience. The centre of the operatic world in his day was Paris, where as a young man he had tried without success for more than two years to establish himself. Whether or not he ended up in debtor's prison, as he said he did, there is no question that his spirit was close to broken during those young days in Paris. He was convinced that he had been betrayed by the head of the musical establishment – Giacomo Meyerbeer, a Jew, a French composer with a half-Italian, half-German name and a facile, sure-fire formula for popular success, but not, it now seems clear, a man who deliberately sabotaged Wagner's early efforts. Then, later in life, when he had realized many of his ambitions, Wagner was convinced that the criticism of his works in the press – much of it persistently ignorant criticism – could only be explained by Jewish influence.

There is a good deal of odious ranting in 'Judaism in Music,' and the essay was to be valuable propaganda a century later in the hands of Joseph Goebbels. But Bryan Magee, in *Aspects of Wagner* (the shortest book on Wagner and surely one of the best) notes that 'Judaism in Music' was in one way remarkably perceptive for its time. Something important was beginning in Europe in Wagner's day, and Wagner was, however wrong-headedly, among the first to see it. For the hundred and fifty years since Wagner wrote that pamphlet about Jews having made no contribution to European culture, Jews have made absolutely astonishing contributions to art, science, and thought, 'a renaissance of almost incredible proportions' to which the list of Nobel Prize winners alone will bear testimony, an achievement that 'cannot be matched by the 99½ percent of the human race who are not Jews.'[6] And at least three Jews – Marx, Freud, and Einstein – have had in their separate ways a greater influence on the twentieth century than Wagner, or any artist, has had.

How are we to account for this cultural explosion? Is it that Jews are more gifted than other people? Few Jews would suggest that. Magee notes that they, of all people, should be immune to Master Race theories. What happened was that the Jews of Europe were, after the French Revolution, emerging from centuries of ghettoization, where their traditions and their faith had sustained them, but where the restraints laid oppressively upon them had left them unable to make significant contributions to the cultures of the lands in which they lived. But within two generations after their acceptance into society, and particularly into German-speaking societies, Jews were making extraordinary contributions to art and knowledge.

There have been similar explosions of cultural achievement from other peoples ghettoized in various ways – the Irish, for example, suddenly responsible in the late nineteenth century for the most notable achievements in English literature. Magee notes that it usually takes two generations after the 'liberation' (and sometimes after a period of strident extremism) before the cultural achievements of oppressed minorities begin to appear. Nor is it always a matter of nationality. I confidently expect that we will see remarkable contributions made to our culture in the future by black people, by aboriginal people, and especially, when they too are relieved of the burden of extremist reaction, by that half of the human race who have in some eras made admirable rulers and in recent centuries have given us wonderfully perceptive novels and much else, but most of whom have until recently been denied the privileges of higher education and have never been given real encouragement in creating what, ironically, has often been thought the most feminine of the arts, music.

Wagner did not foresee any cultural explosion happening with the Jews of his day, but he did wonder why it was that the Jews of his day, and for centuries before his day, were sometimes intellectually distinguished but seemed incapable of making important contributions to European culture. It was that perception that fuelled his most notorious pamphlet. By the end of his life, he had to accept the obvious fact that artistic Jews were coming from all sides to help him – singers, conductors, instrumentalists, designers, producers. He was not always respectful of them. But then he was not always respectful of hundreds of others who were of service to him. When a new, panicky anti-Semitism began to spread across Europe, Wagner insisted to the faithful Angelo Neumann, a Jew, that he had 'absolutely no connection' with the movement.[7] He explicitly rejected what was called 'race religion' in his essay 'Heroism and Christianity', and he refused to sign a mass petition against Jews. He may have had self-serving reasons for taking these stands, and it is clear from the diaries kept by Cosima that he followed the growth of anti-Semitism with some interest. But then he followed all developments with interest, and the diaries contain, along with the same bigoted opinions common in most intellectual circles in Wagner's day, many tolerant remarks about individual Jews, and expressions of gratitude to them.

On the other hand, in his pamphlets Wagner also called Jews 'repugnant in appearance' and their language 'gibberish.' He held them responsible for capitalism and thence for all of society's miseries.[8] And – to take one egregious example from among many – a year before he died he made in jest a horrendous remark for which, in the light of later events, it is impossible to forgive him. It was at the time that the newspapers were reporting a fire that had broken out during a performance at the Vienna Court Theatre, in which many people lost their lives. Wagner was asked, in a private conversation, what he thought of Lessing's tolerant play about an admirable Jew, *Nathan der Weise*. Wagner didn't think much of the play, and he replied, 'All Jews should be burned at a performance of *Nathan der Weise*.'[9] Jews, who have suffered more in this century than any other people, must be given complete understanding when, as some do, they cannot forgive Wagner for such remarks. But many Jews *have* been able to overlook them, for they have heard *seriously* intended remarks of the same ilk from other writers, even from men of genius, even from religious leaders. And they know that Wagner often said stupid things, particularly near the end of his life. They know that he had little tolerance for, and indulged in Philoctetes-like rants against, other groups as well. The French, for example: the vulgar disruption of the Paris premiere of his *Tannhäuser* was the greatest musical scandal of the nineteenth century, and Wagner's memory of that, and of his previous humiliation in Paris, rankled all his life and sometimes exploded in savage outbursts. 'How shall we feel,' he wrote to a friend during the Franco-Prussian War, 'when Paris the monstrous is burned to the ground?' Wagner was also unsparing in his contempt for Catholic priests: Cosima records him saying that they should be denied freedom of the press, that their schools should be taken away from them, that all of them should be wiped out, that everyone stirred up by them should be shot down.[10] But it would be a mistake to take the ranting for the whole man.

Nietzsche was the first of many to suggest that Wagner's anti-Semitic statements were really an expression of *self*-hatred, that Wagner feared that his stepfather, Ludwig Geyer, might actually be his real father. And Geyer, Nietzsche added, was a Jewish name. He was wrong:

Ludwig Geyer, the versatile actor who married Wagner's widowed mother, was not a Jew, and in any case prosopological and other evidence indicates pretty conclusively that Wagner was not Geyer's son but the legitimate, last-born child of one Carl Friedrich Wagner, a police actuary with an interest in the theatre. But if Wagner was not himself Jewish, he may well have *thought* that he was, and he sometimes saw himself caricatured as a Jew in the press. His attitude towards Judaism, then, was, as was so much else about him, profoundly ambivalent.

What did Wagner really think should be done with the Jews of Germany? He thought that they should be assimilated into the culture of the country in which they lived – once Germany, still struggling towards national unity in his day, had had the opportunity independently to establish its own culture. The Jews *were* in fact being assimilated in his day, many of them, like Mendelssohn, enthusiastically adopting the traditions of their native countries. Wagner hoped, arrogantly enough, that his own art would help the Jews in this. But he used, in reference to their assimilation, two terms that have been misinterpreted: one was 'redemption,' which has to be understood, not as imputing guilt to the Jewish race, but as Wagner's term for a personal, symbolic death to self, a Schopenhauerian denial of the will – something sought by many of Wagner's characters and something Wagner declared that he needed himself. The other term was 'self-annihilation': it must be insisted that by that term Wagner meant that a Jew had to renounce his ancestral traditions if he was to be assimilated into German culture. The two terms are unfeeling and the second is, today, totally unacceptable, but in no way did it ever mean or even imply 'genocide,' as some critics recently have tried to make it mean.[11]

That brings me to the new problem raised in the last two decades by critics of Wagner – that there is vicious anti-Semitism, not just in the prose writings, but in the operas themselves. I shall not burden you with the names of these undisciplined critics, who choose, as the Nazis themselves once did, to consider only what in Wagner serves their purposes. I shall not attempt here to refute them one by one. But let it be said that, while there are passages in Wagner's political essays, and statements made in private conversations, that are anti-Semitic in tone, he wrote hundreds of pages explaining his operas, and never once did he make a statement there to indicate, even slightly, that they, or their characters, or their situations, were intended as anti-Semitic.[12] He did compare Kundry in *Parsifal* to the mythic Wandering Jew, but sympathetically, and in any case Wagner's Kundry is a character who functions on several levels, perhaps most importantly as a neo-Buddhist portrayal of 'the eternal return.' The new Wagner critics insist that Beckmesser, the town clerk in *Die Meistersinger*, is a Jewish caricature, and his singing a parody of a synagogue cantor; but, 'quite apart from the fact that, in their professional status and social roles, town clerks and Jews were never one and the same'[13] in sixteenth-century Germany, Sixtus Beckmesser (certainly an 'echt-sounding German name')[14] must for the purposes of *Die Meistersinger* stand for the finicky German pedant familiar to most of us in academe. Beckmesser becomes the

subject of ridicule in Wagner's comedy not because
Wagner thought him a Jew, but because (as any classical
scholar can tell you) comedy from its origins – and Wagner read deeply into those origins – has demanded a figure of fun, an *alazon*, a *miles gloriosus* from within society
on whose correction the survival of society depends. It is
a measure of the arrogance of the new Wagner critics
that one of them, who thinks he has conclusively proven
Beckmesser to be a Jewish caricature, now insists that
henceforth no production of *Die Meistersinger* can be
valid unless it depicts his so-called findings on stage.[15]

Wagner cannot, in the end, be completely exonerated
for what happened in Nazi Germany. It is not a matter of
Hitler being spellbound by Wagner's music. Millions of
people, good people, have been spellbound by Wagner's
music. It is a matter of ideas having consequences. The
anti-Semitic statements in Wagner's prose writings were
extremely useful to the Nazis, especially when, for propaganda purposes, they could be broadcast to the
accompaniment of some of the most persuasive music
ever written. But that music was not designed for those
purposes. It has not yet been demonstrated that the
operas are anti-Semitic, and I doubt if it ever will be, or
can be. Critics who insist that Wagner's is the music of
storm troopers, new productions that ignore the mythic
dimension of his works and turn the works into harbin-
gers of concentration-camp cruelty, are actually accepting 'the perverse interpretations [of those works] propagated by the Nazis.'[16]

The deconstruction of Wagner and his operas will
likely continue as long as deconstructionism haunts the

halls of this and other universities. Meanwhile, I shall let
two Jewish voices speak finally to this matter. One is that
dauntless writer and teacher, Joseph Horowitz. He spoke
at a symposium on Wagner and the Jews held this past
summer at the Wagner festival in Bayreuth, and there he
charged the new anti-Wagner critics with ignoring completely 'that part of Wagner that speaks to Jews.' Of the
figures claimed to be hateful Jewish caricatures or worse,
Horowitz argued that Wagner understood Kundry 'compassionately,' that Beckmesser 'invites compassion,' that
Alberich, whom an anti-Wagner critic recently called 'a
revolting Jewish *schlemiel*' was thought, by one of today's
leading conductors, to be 'the most compassionately
drawn' of all the figures in the *Ring*.[17] The characters,
Horowitz insisted, are not anti-Jewish stereotypes.

The second voice is Leonard Bernstein, who speaks
not for Wagner's characters but simply for the acceptance of his music. In a piece in the *New York Times* enti-
tled 'Wagner's Music Isn't Racist,' Bernstein wrote,
'Wagner is long dead and buried, as is the Third Reich,
but we music lovers are alive and hungry for great
music. And if Wagner wrote great music, as I think he
did, why should we not embrace it fully and be nourished by it?'[18]

Nourished by it ... I'd like now to talk, with some relief,
about something far less often commented on – the enor-
mous and very real *positive* influence Wagner's art has
had on the century now hurrying to its end. And I shall
base my discussion largely on two works of literature of
unquestioned importance – one written by a French Jew

and the other by an Anglo-Catholic whose work is now (I hope, only temporarily) disparaged, like Wagner's, for being anti-Semitic.

The poem that, to my generation in college, best spoke for our century was T.S. Eliot's *The Waste Land*. I remember that there were well-thumbed copies of it strewn about Trinity College back in the forties. At St Michael's College, in the days of Marshall McLuhan, we students eagerly organized our own seminars to discuss it outside of class. Even the engineers on this campus knew it and cited it. It was our poem, even if we didn't understand every grim prophecy made in its maze of quotations.

The Waste Land, emblematic of so much in our century, contains two direct quotations from *Tristan und Isolde*, two quotations from the *Ring*, and, as Professor William Blissett of this university has pointed out, many subtle echoes of *Parsifal* as well: even the familiar opening, 'April is the cruelest month' (cruel because it holds the promise of rebirth), can be related, via Eliot's reference to the Starnbergersee where Wagner's patron Ludwig II was drowned, to the Good Friday scene in *Parsifal*.[19]

That Eliot quotes strikingly from Wagner in perhaps the most famous poem of our century does not of itself speak of a pervasive Wagnerian influence. Eliot quotes from any number of other figures: *The Waste Land* is a depiction of Western civilization in decay, reduced to butt-ends, to fragments of Sappho, St Augustine, and Shakespeare shored up against the winds of twentieth-century change. The West is going under. Only the Eastern thunder of the Upanishads speaks peace. Soon it will all be over. We're closing up the pub. Eliot telegraphs that headline throughout the poem in unpunctuated capital letters: HURRY UP PLEASE ITS TIME.

But of all the figures of Western civilization, from Petronius to Jessie Weston, quoted in the poem, Wagner is the most central to its themes. He too saw Western civilization as headed for disaster: he ended his four-part drama about the Nibelungs with a world-destruction myth that was not part of his sources. And, as Eliot perceived, Wagner thought that Eastern wisdom could save the West. He patterned, not just the end of the *Ring*, but much of *Tristan* and *Parsifal* on Buddhist teachings.

But that is not the end of Wagner's influence on *The Waste Land*. The music of Wagner's operas, especially from the *Ring* onwards, is largely composed from leitmotifs or, as Wagner called them, *Gedächtnismotive*, 'motifs of memory' – recurrent fragments of music ranging from two notes to not much more than twelve, associated at first with personages or objects or actions but by the end of the fifteen-hour cycle charged with additional meanings through their repeated interaction with one another. That is what is going on in *The Waste Land* as in no poetry since the patterned, shifting, interacting images in the choral odes of Aeschylus. Wagner knew Aeschylus. He read him constantly while composing the *Ring*, and he fashioned a new kind of musical composition after the Greek's poetic techniques. Eliot in turn knew Wagner, and fashioned a new kind of poetic composition after the German's musical techniques. It was that haunting, allusive, essentially Wagnerian use of quotations in *The Waste Land* that caught the imagination of my student generation at this university, and indeed of the civilized world.

Marcel Proust knew about Wagner's motifs of memory, too, and wrote a new kind of novel, the seven-part *À la Recherche du temps perdu*, out of motifs in his memory that, constantly recurring, have by the novel's end taken on almost innumerable associations. But that is hardly all that is Wagnerian about Proust's voluminous work, the vastest and perhaps the greatest novel of our century. Its title means something like *On the Quest for Lost Time*. Its narrator seeks to recover the past – seemingly lost and irrecoverable. He seeks even to redeem time from its endless onward flow as he shifts back and forth between present and past – recapturing his experiences before they are lost in the recesses of memory, examining them and their interrelationships and discovering meaning in them.

The inspiration for this 'stream of consciousness' writing came almost surely from the third act of the opera we spoke of at the beginning of this lecture, *Tristan und Isolde* – from the very act that our professor of French literature found unendurable. In the passage from Proust that everyone knows best, the narrator, named Marcel for Proust himself, dips a bit of cake, the now-famous 'petite madeleine,' into a cup of tea, and evokes a complex series of emotions. He puts down his cup and retraces his thoughts to the moment when, as a boy, he sipped his first spoonful of tea. He resolutely dismisses all other concerns to concentrate on that memory: on Sunday morning in his native village of Combray, when he visited his Aunt Léonie upstairs in her bedroom, she would give him a little piece of madeleine dipped in tea. And, with that incident remembered, recaptured from his memory, the narrator's whole past begins to flood in on him – the old grey house, the street, the lost childhood that could never really be lost, his attachment to his mother, the visits paid to his family by their neighbour Swann, the clatter of the little bell on the garden gate as Swann left the house – a stream of stored-up associations that, with repetitions, modulations, and cross-references, eventually enables the narrator to see how the mind remembers, and to re-evaluate the present shallow surfaces of his own life and those of his society

If you visit Iliers-Combray today, you will find devout Proustians retracing the author's steps from the old grey house (where, in Aunt Léonie's bedroom, a fresh madeleine is placed by her teacup every day) through the garden gate with its clapping bell, across those other sources of memory, the water lilies and hyacinth bushes where Swann walked. Tourists will also attempt to find there the much longer, alternate walk of Proust's childhood, the longer path he called the Guermantes way. Then they'll hasten off to the seaside town of Cabourg, to see the places where young Marcel was tempted by the *jeunes filles en fleurs*, and thence to Paris to visit the salons of the wealthy and powerful from which, aided by his memories, Proust ripped the masks off a glittering and utterly false society.

Compare Proust's recovered memories with those of Tristan in the third act of Wagner's opera. The wounded hero has been transported to his ancestral Kareol, where he spent his childhood, and wakens out of unconsciousness to the mournful sound of a shepherd's pipe. As he gazes across the waste sea that Eliot was to remember in

The Waste Land, he muses on the other world he has seen deep in his unconscious, a dark land of wonder that he longed to share with Isolde. His longing for her to join him there has driven him upwards to consciousness to find her and bring her back with him, out of the false world of glitter, power, and prestige to the real world he has found in his unconscious. As the past and the present blur in his memory, Tristan imagines he sees Isolde's ship coming on the sea – only to hear the shepherd's mournful tune insist that the sea is still 'waste and desolate.'

Then, a half-century before Freud and Jung, Tristan embarks on a second quest, through a deeper cycle of memory, a leitmotivic journey in which he affirms the reality of the unconscious world within *over* that of the conscious world without. As the shepherd's nostalgic piping comes sadly floating to his ears once again, Tristan explores his unconscious. He remembers how the same shepherd's tune hung on the evening air when, as a boy, he first heard that his father had died before he was born, and how it sounded again, in the early morning, when they told him that his mother had died giving him birth.

Here is where Sir Colin Davis said, 'When you're conducting it, it's just touch and go. You're just holding on. It's so overwhelming.' And here is where our great Canadian tenor, Jon Vickers, grappled on stage with what one critic called 'Titanic impulses,' calling up 'memorial yearnings, ancient griefs and triumph dug from the collective unconscious' of us all, in a performance that was 'like a giant sculpture on which the hammer strokes are still visible.' Another critic, hearing Mr Vickers do this scene on records, called his performance 'absolutely authentic ... something unique as if the story were, just this once, literally true.' Then he added, to show how intense and unnerving the experience had been for him: 'I can pay no higher tribute; but I never want to hear it again.' Those who know *Tristan* will know what he meant. The work is almost unendurable in a great performance, and Jon Vickers's performance was certainly that.[20]

The wounded, haunted Tristan comes painfully to see that the human condition, inherited from father and mother, nurtured by ambition, intensified by sexual passion, never fulfilled, driving him ever onward, is not the real world, and he summons up all his strength to renounce it. Only then is he is rewarded with a vision of the world that lies beyond the physical − a vision of Isolde coming to him, walking over the sea on waves of flowers. Tristan at that moment has suffered through to what Wagner thought, at that time of his life, was the ultimate human truth, buried deep in the unconscious, but clearly stated in the wisdom of the East − that only when a man renounces his insatiable desires can he find the Nirvana-peace which is his true fulfilment.

Proust was to reach different conclusions in his remembrance of things past, and instead of a shepherd's tune to trigger remembrance he uses that bit of madeleine dipped in tea. But what inspired him to explore past memory came, I think clearly, from that last act of Tristan. It may even be of some significance that when Wagner was writing that act, he received a pack-

age of Zwieback from Mathilde Wesendonck, whose
attentions had inspired the first two acts, and he wrote to
her (admittedly with tongue-in-cheek exclamations) to
say how, when dipped in a little milk, the Zwieback had
solved all his problems of composition. It's a small point,
but I've often wondered whether Proust, who wrote
famously of the bit of cake dipped in tea, knew of Wagner's dry biscuit dipped in milk. One can never be too
sure where the influence of Wagner ends when it comes
to important works of twentieth-century art.[21]

Proust never openly acknowledged the influence of
Tristan on his novel. But he seems to have paid a graceful
tribute to Wagner when he named the first three parts of
On the Quest for Lost Time 'Swann's Way,' 'Mid a Budding
Grove' (that is to say, 'À l'Ombre des jeune filles en
fleurs'), and 'The Guermantes Way.' For in *Parsifal*, Wagner's opera on the quest for the lost Grail, we see, in Act
I, the hero following a swan's flight to the castle of the
Holy Grail, in Act II, his awaking to memories of his
mother in an encounter in a garden with mythic flower
maidens, and, in Act III, his restoration of the Grail after
tracing the long way back to the waiting figure of
Gurnemanz.

It would be easy to detail the influence of Wagner on
other French literature in the latter part of the nineteenth
century and into the twentieth, for Verlaine and Mal-
larmé were ardent in their praise and imitation of him,
and French intellectuals founded their own *Revue Wagnérienne* for imagists, symbolists, novelists,[22] and turn-of-
the century decadents. As for other literatures, those
devout readers of James Joyce's *Ulysses* making their pil-

grimages through Dublin's streets are following a quest mapped out in Homer's *Odyssey,* of course – but it is also a quest in which meanings accrue through a hundred recurrent leitmotifs, à la Wagner. *Finnegan's Wake* too is a vast crazy-quilt of leitmotivic language, and William Blissett has shown how the unforgettable climactic phrase of Joyce's *Portrait of the Artist as a Young Man* ('to forge in the smithy of my soul the uncreated conscience of my race') is shaped and signified not just from Yeats but, via Nietzsche's *Beyond Good and Evil*, from the coming-of-age of Wagner's young Siegfried, forging his sword. And Gabriele D'Annunzio's *Trionfo della Morte* (1894), George Moore's *Evelyn Innes* (1898), Joseph Conrad's *Nostromo* (1904), Thomas Mann's 'Tristan' (1903) and 'Wälsungenblut' (1905), E.M. Forster's 'The Celestial Omnibus' (1903) and *The Longest Journey* (1907), D.H. Lawrence's *The Trespasser* (1912), Willa Cather's wonderful *The Song of the Lark* (1915) and *Youth and the Bright Medusa* (1921), Virginia Woolf's *To the Lighthouse* (1927) and *The Waves* (1931), and even Bernard Malamud's baseball story *The Natural* (1952) are a few more of the fictional works of the past hundred years which critics have seen as influenced, in their themes and/or their leitmotivic structures, by Wagner.[23]

Recently, we who taught classics at this university had to rethink our courses in mythology along new lines established by Claude Levi-Strauss and his structuralism. But Levi-Strauss himself saw Wagner as the father of his structural analysis of myth, and declared the line Wagner's Gurnemanz speaks to Parsifal as they make their way to the temple of the Holy Grail – 'You see, my

son, time becomes space here' – the most profound of all
definitions of myth. Wagner chose myth for the subject
matter of six of his greatest operas because, as he said
often enough, myth was timeless, intuitive, profound,
and concerned not with the particular but with the uni-
versal. Medievalists used to say (and to some extent still
say) that Wagner wilfully distorted the myths of the Middle Ages. But it has recently been suggested, persua-
sively, that Wagner, in *Tristan*, the *Ring*, and *Parsifal*,
thought and felt his way back beyond his Christian
sources to what we now see as the original meaning of
the myths.[24] He mined the myths for all the truth he
could find in them. He saw myth as a revelation of what
transpires in the human soul, and he used it as prophecy:
the *Ring*, which began as a parable of Europe's evolution
towards a classless, progressive society, eventually
became (at the start) a parable of the evolution of primitive man into consciousness and (at the close) a predic-
tion that man was meant to evolve beyond the state of
consciousness which has been his thus far in recorded
history. As Wagner laboured through twenty-five years
over his vast Nibelungen project, changing its ending six
times, 'an intuitive idea kept hammering away at him ...
perhaps the most important idea of his century, and not
to be fulfilled for centuries to come, though man's myths
knew ... [that] it would someday happen: *man was meant
to evolve beyond his present state*, even as he had evolved
into it.'[25] The *Ring*, a saga of struggle, of incomprehensible loss, of death and rebirth, is equally about the
powerful forces of nature wondered at by primitive man
and about the unfathomed forces battling within the soul

of each conscious individual at the current state of our evolutionary development. It is the story of a soul writ large, the most astonishing mining of myth since Aeschylus.

Just two instances, from among many, of Wagner's influence in the world of painting: Vincent Van Gogh wrote to his brother Theo, 'I am reading a book on Wagner. What an artist! One like that in painting would be something. It *will* come.' And again to the faithful Theo, 'I made a vain attempt to learn music, so much did I already feel the relation between our colour and Wagner's music.'[25] Wassily Kandinsky said there were two events in his youth which were to stamp his entire life – an exhibition of impressionist paintings and a performance of *Lohengrin*. He thought Wagner's music 'a challenge to his art,' for it 'conveyed intense visual experience more powerfully than any painting,'[27] and indeed no painting I know conveys the shimmering intensity of *Tristan*'s 'Liebesnacht' so uncannily as does Kandinsky's 1906 colour drawing *Die Nacht*.

In music, the great composers after Wagner have either followed his lead (Richard Strauss, Bruckner, Mahler, Schoenberg, Berg, the young Sibelius, the *Parsifal*-loving Elgar, the *Parsifal*-smitten Puccini), or else, like Stravinsky, have of set purpose swum against the Wagnerian current. The innovating Debussy, ambivalent about Wagner, succumbed, in his one complete opera, to Wagner's influence even while attempting to avoid it, virtually quoting from *Parsifal* in several passages of *Pelléas* et *Mélisande*. Wagner has also influenced the way music, and not just his own music, is performed: he was the first to darken an auditorium during a performance, the first to introduce much of modern stagecraft, the first to have sunk the orchestra into a pit, the first in the great line of central European conductors that continued from his immediate disciples Mottl and Richter through to – to name only the greatest – Furtwängler, Bruno Walter, Solti (both of them Jewish), and von Karajan. Meanwhile, the composers of today's 'avant-garde aesthetic'[28] have returned to myth as the proper subject for opera: Karl-Heinz Stockhausen is currently half-way through a massive work called *Licht*, a *Ring*-like cycle of seven operas that depicts the seven-day creation of the world. It is perhaps our contemporary equivalent of Bernard Shaw's most ambitious project, *Back to Methuselah*, which Shaw, a self-confessed 'perfect Wagnerite,' thought of as his own 'Niblung's *Ring*.'

In dance, Diaghilev used the aesthetic principles Wagner had proclaimed in his prose works in an attempt to unify Russian culture. (Not everything in those prose pamphlets is ranting.) Other artists in Diaghilev's country mixed Wagner's ideas into what David Large has called 'a distinctly Russian blend of mysticism, neo-popularism and revolutionary activism.'[29] Sergei Eisenstein, auteur director of *Potemkin* and other famous films on the Russian revolution, learned some of his craft from directing Wagner's *Die Walküre* in the theatre.

And that brings us round again to politics, and to Germany, where – this ought to be said more often – reactions to Wagner have not always been worshipful. Quite the contrary. Bismarck pointedly refused Wagner any financial support (and Wagner, in despair that his work would ever become a source of German renewal, contemplated moving to Minnesota, a freer land where he thought his work might be more appreciated). German interest in Wagner and in his theatre at Bayreuth actually declined during the Weimar Republic. It only revived when it became clear that some ideas in Wagner's prose pamphlets, trumpeted forth by his music, would be ideal propaganda for, indeed provide a powerful mystique for, the ascendent Führer. Even then, Wagner's son Siegfried, in charge of the Bayreuth festival, was outraged by Nazi demonstrations there, made a special point of employing Jewish singers and musicians there, and asked Hitler to stay away from the performances – which he did for eight years. But inevitably, in 1933, with Nazi power established, with Siegfried Wagner dead, and with his widow an intimate friend of Hitler, the Wagner festival became an instrument of Nazi propaganda – and Wagner's name and music became for years to come a symbol for the most inhuman horrors of the century.

Meanwhile, consider this. Theodor Herzl, the founder of modern political Zionism, wrote his manifesto 'The Jewish State' after seeing a performance of *Tannhäuser* in Vienna. He identified strongly with Wagner's outcast hero.

I hope I have shown that, while Wagner's influence on National Socialism in Germany was real, it is by no means all that Wagner can and should signify to us as the century ends. His influence on the foremost figures in the arts, and on many beyond the arts, is no longer a matter of debate. There will always be some who will resist his music, who will find it – as its Philoctetes-composer was – arrogant, driven, manic in its overstatement. Nietzsche once said to Wagner, 'Apparently you think that *all* music ... must leap out of the wall and shake the listener to his very intestines.'[30] But even Nietzsche, at some times Wagner's severest critic, changed his mind about the music many times. After he heard the hushed vision of the Holy Grail in the prelude to *Parsifal*, he wrote, quoting from the last page of Goethe's *Faust*, that he had felt 'a sublime and extraordinary feeling ... an event of the soul ... an awful severity of judgement *von oben*, from on high which ... sees through the soul, piercing it as with knives.'[31] Or, I would say, as with Philoctetes' arrows.

And there, with the prelude to *Parsifal*, is the thought that I'd like to leave you with this evening: Wagner's art cannot be comprehended reductively, with the attention fixed on any one single aspect. It is manifold, many-layered, and many-splendoured. Reactions to it have always varied, and will likely always vary, with the perceptions of the listener. Wagner's art, in short, is like the Grail he depicted in that visionary prelude to *Parsifal*. The Grail of legend affected the knights who quested for it in different ways: some drew sustenance from it, some were sent by it to do great deeds in the world, while some failed utterly to understand it, and some could not see it, even when in its presence. But in every case, the Grail showed them their very selves. And if knowing oneself is the beginning of wisdom – and I think it is – then Wagner's ambivalent and astonishing art is something we need, and shall always need.

NOTES

1 Magee 1988 [1968], 56.

2 Cosima Wagner's diaries, entry for 7 April 1879.

3 I beg the reader's indulgence for repeating this incident, already reported in Lee 1998, 119.

4 William Blissett, writing to me privately, observed: 'Anti-Semitism was not in Wagner's time seen to be a moral failing, as it most assuredly is now, and racial doctrines were elaborated in all innocency by upright characters like Matthew Arnold.'

5 Quoted in Magee 1988 [1968], 24. Deathridge, in Deathridge and Dahlhaus 1984, 81, rightly observes that 'in Mendelssohn, Wagner detected a naturalness and effortlessness of purely musical logic of which he often felt the lack in himself.'

6 Magee 1988 [1968], 19–20. Much the same observation was made by the Jewish pianist David Bar-Illan, in Dubal 1984, 66–7: 'For 1800 years, while the Jews were ghettoized, I think they must have stored up tremendous amounts of intellectual and artistic energy. When the Jews started to assimilate into European society around 1850, that emancipation brought a flood of thought and artistic achievement ... Before this the Jew could only pour his heart and mind into the *Talmud* and the *Torah*.'

7 Letter of 23 February 1881. In Spencer and Millington 1987, 906.

8 Remarks made mainly in 'Judaism in Music,' reported by Kühnel in Müller and Wapnewski 1992, 597.

9 Cosima Wagner's diaries, entry for 18 December 1881. Sabor, who is too forgiving, notes as well that Wagner, when he lost a manuscript in the mail, said playfully, 'This could only have happened to me. I am positive the Jews caused my manuscript to be stolen' (Sabor 1987, 179).

10 Cosima Wagner's diaries, entry for 27 April 1870.

11 The best discussion of this vexed matter is Borchmeier 1992, 172–6.

12 One of the critics, faced with a barrage of sensible objections to his book, issued a sort of *recusatio* in the paperback edition: apparently he did not wish to say that Alberich, Mime, Hagen, Beck-

messer, and Klingsor were 'only, unequivocably, or nothing more
than Jews.' He intended to say that his was 'one of the many
potential credible interpretations that co-exist within the *reception*
of these works' (emphasis mine). Quoted from a review of the
revised edition of the critic's book in *Opera Now*, November/
December 1997, 103.

13 Borchmeier 1992, 183.

14 Vaget 1993, 227.

15 The one possibly valid point this critic makes, that the reference to
the 'Dornenhecke' in Walther's trial song would call to some German minds an anti-Semitic story ('The Jew in the Brambles') preserved in the Brothers Grimm, hardly establishes that there is an
anti-Semitic coding in the opera as a whole. See Vaget 1993, 227–
32 for a proper assessment of the matter. As for the 'notorious'
passage sung by Hans Sachs near the close of *Die Meistersinger*,
about the necessity of preserving 'holy German art' from foreign
influences, Thomas Mann (in Marek 1957, 356–7) says, 'It is pre-
cisely these lines ... that attest the intellectuality of Wagner's
nationalism and its remoteness from the political sphere; they
betray a complete anarchic indifference to the state, so long as the
spiritually German, the "Deutsche Kunst", survives.' The lines
actually *reject* military might and assert instead the primary
importance of art for national survival.

16 Magee 1988 [1968], 44.

17 Horowitz 1998, 17. He says, with reference to another supposed
caricature, 'The most "Jewish" portrayal of Mime known to me –
Heinz Zednik's in the 1976 Patrice Chereau *Ring* – also proved the
most human and sympathetic.' I have certainly seen performances
of *Parsifal* in which Kundry of all the characters made the most
overwhelmingly sympathetic impression, and performances of
Die Meistersinger in which Beckmesser stole the show.

18 Bernstein 1991. From a posthumously published article in the *New
York Times*, excerpted from a script written and filmed on the occa-
sion of Bernstein's conducting an all-Wagner program at the
Wiener Staatsoper in 1985.

19 Blissett 1978, 71–5.

20 The two critics quoted are Cairns 1973, 146, and Holloway 1979, 370.

21 The Zwieback incident is discussed in Weiner 1980, 679–84.

22 Édouard Dejardins, who wrote what is thought, even by Joyce, to be the first stream-of-consciousness novel, *Les Lauriers sont coupées* (1888), was for many years the editor of the *Revue Wagnérienne*. Émile Zola, naturalist though he was, wrote, about the 'repetitions' in his novels: 'This is a literary device that I began by using with some timidity, but have since pushed perhaps to excess. In my view it gives more body to a work, and strengthens its unity. The device is somewhat akin to the motifs of Wagner, and if you will ask some musical friends of yours to explain his use of these, you will understand pretty well my use of the device in literature' (quoted from Blissett 1963, 239–40).

23 The Nietzschean hero of D'Annunzio's *Il Trionfo della Morte* recounts in his memory (through some seventeen pages) the performance of *Tristan* he saw at Bayreuth, and then leaps to his death, taking his mistress with him. Wagner appears briefly as a character in the same author's *Il Fuoco*, and his presence overshadows the whole of that Venice-set novel. Wagner's work, especially *Parsifal*, dominates the world of Moore's *Evelyn Innes*, its characters and discussions. Conrad's comment on his *Nostromo* ('Silver is the pivot of the moral and material events, affecting the lives of everybody in the tale') was bound to remind critics of the gold in Wagner's *Ring*: Keith Carabine (1984, xii) says, 'As all the characters respond to [the silver mine's] power and fall under its influence, as they use and interpret it, they wittingly or unwittingly disclose their deepest needs and purposes whether spiritual, emotional, material or political.' Siegmund and Sieglinde are the names of the incestuous siblings who attend a performance of *Die Walküre* in Thomas Mann's 'Wälsungenblut,' while *Tristan*'s music figures largely in Mann's story of that name, and there is hardly any fictional work of Mann that does not bear some Wagnerian imprint, thematic, leitmotivic, or both. The boy in Forster's 'Celestial Omnibus' and the young man in his almost autobiographical *Longest Journey* are fascinated by the rainbow bridge in *Das Rhein-*

gold. The first draft of D.H. Lawrence's early *The Trespasser* was called *The Saga of Siegmund*, and its illicit lovers were named Siegmund and Sieglinde; in the final draft the doomed hero is still called Siegmund and Lawrence's *Tristan*-like narrative is liberally sprinkled with allusions to Wagner. Wagner is essential to understanding the protagonists of Cather's *Song of the Lark* and of several stories in her *Medusa*. Virginia Woolf visited Bayreuth early in her career and wrote 'Impressions' of the festival for the London *Times* in 1909. Her *To the Lighthouse*, structured like *Parsifal*, is a narrative woven largely of leitmotivic images. In her Wagnerian *The Waves*, narrative is largely dispensed with and the fluctuating lives of the six characters who remember the central figure, Percival, are detailed almost completely in terms of leitmotifs. The 'Wagnerian' themes some have found in *The Natural* are more likely drawn from the whole fund of Grail stories; Malamud calls his ball club 'the Knights' and his Parsifal figure 'Roy.' But scattered incidents in the narrative do suggest elements of *Tannhäuser* and the *Ring* as well as Wagner's Grail operas. For much more about Wagner's importance to twentieth-century writers see the bibliography entries under Blissett, a subtle and persuasive Wagnerian. Furness (1992, 396–8), notes still further instances of Wagner's impact on literature, and ends with the oracular statement, 'He has conquered vast areas of the world's mind, and the canon of modern classics is beholden to his hegemony.'

24 See Rougement 1939; Lee 1990, esp. 93–7; and Jackson Knight 1936, 143–4.
25 Lee 1990, 95.
26 Quoted in Hall 1992, 398 and 400.
27 Quoted in Hall 1992, 400.
28 The phrase is from Whittall 1992, 395, the source of some my observations here on music.
29 Large 1992, 387.
30 Quoted in Magee 1988 [1968], 40.
31 Quoted in Beckett 1981, 115.

CHAPTER THREE

You Use Works of Art to See Your Soul

With this lecture we bring to an end our three-evening examination of Wagner, and I should say at this point that, even with the time generously allotted me by the Larkin-Stuart committee, I haven't found room to do more than touch on many matters that I should have liked to speak of in detail. Because my mandate was to speak mainly on ethical concerns, I haven't done much more than allude to how Wagner introduced into drama a whole dimension that was unavailable to other great dramatists – an omniscient orchestra that, through leitmotifs, constantly comments on the action, that tells us what the characters on stage do not say, and sometimes do not even know, that limns for us their unexpressed desires, doubts, loves, and fears. I haven't been able to defend the thesis that thereby Wagner raised drama to a degree of expressiveness beyond the reach of any other dramatist of the sung or spoken word.[1] I haven't even mentioned that Wagner the poet wrote the text of each opera in a verse form radically different from that of the others, and one in every case admirably suited to the new matter at hand. Or how he gave each separate opera its own distinct instrumentation and sound – from the A-major silvery-blue beauty of *Lohengrin* to *Tristan*'s surging chromaticism to the diatonic C-major ripeness of *Die Meistersinger* to the luxuriant strings and sounding brass of the *Ring* to the stained-glass transparencies of *Parsifal*. And I haven't spoken of any of the operas in detail. Not, that is, until now.

In this lecture, partly to substantiate the observations of our two previous evenings, we shall concentrate on one of Wagner's operas, and that opera will be ... none of those I've just mentioned. I have chosen for discussion Wagner's earlier *Tannhäuser*. You may rightly think that one of Wagner's more mature operas would better illustrate the points I have made over the past two evenings. But I have lectured in Toronto recently on *Tristan*, *Die Meistersinger*, and *Parsifal*, my *Lohengrin* comments are newly available on CD and audio cassette from the Met Guild, and my book on the *Ring* is still selling. So the early *Tannhäuser* it shall be. It needs talking about here, for it is unquestionably a great work, and it hasn't been done in Toronto in more than sixty years.

Begun when Wagner was in his late twenties, *Tannhäuser* was given its premiere in Dresden in 1845, and was revised (with extensive changes in the first act especially) for Paris sixteen years later. Between those two versions of *Tannhäuser* Wagner wrote *Lohengrin*, *Das Rheingold*, *Die Walküre*, two acts of *Siegfried*, and all of *Tristan und Isolde*. So *Tannhäuser* as performed today in the customary Paris version is a curious hybrid – part youthful and relatively unsophisticated, part mid-career and harmonically complex.

Even with the later additions and refinements, however, it remains a young man's opera, and for the young it can come as a kind of revelation. *Tannhäuser*, for anyone who surrenders to its spell, tells one something about one's own self – especially of one's young self.

It was the first opera I ever heard, on a Met broadcast in 1942, and, as I have said both on the air and in print,[2] it left me, at age eleven, at a whole new level of awareness, astonished at the response that music could awaken in me. Eduard Hanslick was twice that age, twenty-two,

when he first heard *Tannhäuser*. Though he was one day
to become Wagner's arch-critic, what he heard that
evening was 'a musical experience carrying the listener
irresistibly with it, in such a way that what occurred in
the orchestra and on the stage became part of his own
life.'[3] Baudelaire was not so young – well on into his thir-
ties – when he first heard the *Tannhäuser* overture. But his
response was much the same: 'What I felt was indescribable ... I already knew this music. It seemed to me that
this was my music.' He wrote to Wagner to say, 'Thank
you ... You have brought me back in touch with myself.'[4]

Wagner himself looked back on the creation of *Tannhäuser* and said much the same thing as the rest of us
about it: 'As I sketched the music, and brought it to com-
pletion, I was consumed by a sensual excitement that
held my blood and nerves at fever pitch. My true nature
... was completely restored to me. I thought that with this
work I had signed my death sentence ... I could hope no
more for life. I felt that.'[5]

The music may have come in a rush of excitement, but
as always Wagner wrote the text first, and he had a
tougher time with that. It is worth going into this matter
for a moment, just to show how the literary Wagner
worked. The text of his *Tannhäuser* conflates two German
legends which were originally quite unrelated. The first,
preserved for us in a fifteenth-century poem called the
Tannhäuserlied and in the *Deutsche Sagen* of the Brothers
Grimm, tells how a medieval minstrel-knight named
Tannhäuser (perhaps, 'forest-dweller') dallied for a time
with the pagan goddess Venus in her underworld grotto,
the Venusberg, but eventually grew weary of voluptuous

pursuits and asked to return to the world above. (In one version Venus actually imprisoned Tannhäuser below to keep him with her.) Eventually he called for help to the Virgin Mary, was released by the Virgin's power, and then travelled to Rome to ask the Pope's forgiveness for his carnal sins. The Pope's response, however, was, 'When this staff that I hold in my hands bears new green branches, only then will your sins be taken away, and not before.' So the despairing Tannhäuser returned to Venus, to await the day of the last judgment, when God himself might perhaps give him a more merciful sentence. Meanwhile, God sent a sign of his forgiveness by causing the Pope's staff, on the third day, miraculously to put out green shoots.

Wagner made a change or two in this folk material. The old tale rather clearly reflects the increasing disaffection medieval Germany felt for the papacy. But when Wagner's opera was first performed, his enemies in Dresden accused him of accepting money from Catholic circles to glorify the papacy: for in the opera the Pope's burgeoning staff is brought to Germany by pilgrims just as Wagner's hero, rejecting Venus, dies redeemed by a Catholic saint. And thereby hangs our second tale – the singing contest.

For the middle of his opera, Wagner used a quite separate legend, not a part of the Tannhäuser cycle at all, but preserved in various versions in a Middle High German poem, in the Brothers Grimm, in the tales of E.T.A. Hoffmann, and in a famous eighteenth-century novel by Novalis. (Actually Wagner had about a dozen sources – including Eichendorff, Tieck, and Heine – from which to put his two stories together, and he describes his busying about with the old poems rhapsodically in his essays and letters.) This second story appears to be based on an actual happening. Singing contests used to take place at the court of the Landgraf of Thuringia, in his cliffed and commanding castle, the still lovingly preserved Wartburg, looming over the town of Eisenach. The minstrel knights who participated in the competitions there were known as Minnesingers (singers of courtly love). Wagner puts six of them on the stage, and their names are well known to students of German: Wolfram von Eschenbach, author of the German epic on Parzifal; Walther von der Vogelweide, the best-loved medieval German lyric poet; Reinmar von Zweter, a lyric poet who quarrelled with Walther; Johannes Biterolf; Heinrich der Schreiber; and, most important of all, Heinrich von Ofterdingen. The story went that, when these famous singers were assembled at the Wartburg from all parts of Germany, Heinrich von Ofterdingen defeated them all so handily that they thought he was in league with Satan and challenged him at swordpoint to name the secret of his skill – whereupon he vanished in a puff of sulphurous smoke. Well, Wagner, following suggestions in some earlier Romantic writers, identified Tannhäuser (the sensual lover in one story) with Heinrich (the demonic minstrel in the other). That is why – in case you have wondered – whenever Tannhäuser is addressed in the opera, he is called Heinrich. The double source of Wagner's opera is also reflected in its full title: *Tannhäuser und der Sängerkrieg auf Wartburg,* (*Tannhäuser and the Singer's Contest at the Wartburg*).

We said that there was a Catholic saint involved. And

now all this *Quellenforschung* gets a little complicated. In the old stories the demonic figure who gave Heinrich/ Tannhäuser his secret musical power was a Hungarian magician named Klingsor (the same villain to appear later in Wagner's *Parsifal*). Klingsor, in the old poems, once fled from the Wartburg song contest on a snorting black steed after announcing that a princess had been born at the royal court in Hungary over whom his magic would have no power. She would grow up and marry into the German court of the Wartburg. Well, if you visit the Wartburg today (and I hope some day you will), you will see not just the hall of song where the contests were held, not just the room where centuries later Luther, hiding from the papacy, began his translation of the Bible into German and threw his inkwell at the devil, but a series of delicate frescoes that tell the many legends of this good princess. For she was a historical person – Saint Elisabeth of Hungary. Liszt, good Hungarian that he was, wrote an oratorio about her. When I was organist at Holy Rosary Church here in Toronto fifty years ago I used to slip a little of her Wagner music into the Masses on St Elisabeth's day. And when I was in Budapest I said a quiet Mass in her church there.

The historical Elisabeth came from Hungary to marry Landgraf Hermann's son, to live in the Wartburg and do many kind and beautiful things in the castle and in the town below, before her death at the age of twenty-four. She was said to have worked miracles through her prayers. She was too good for Wagner *not* to use. So he advanced her birth slightly and introduced her into his opera as the Landgraf's virgin niece. And he arranged it so that, through her prayers, the debauched minstrel Tannhäuser would be saved from the other minstrels' swords at the Wartburg and saved as well from damnation in the Venusberg.

The more one pokes around in the sources, the more fascinated one becomes, and we can understand Wagner's enthusiasm once he embarked on his subject. For example, he shaped his materials so that the action of the opera shifts back and forth between two hills in what is still called 'the green heart of Germany' – Thuringia. One of these hills is, of course, the hill crowned with the Wartburg, above the town of Eisenach, where Bach was born. The young Wagner once stopped at the lofty castle, a perennial haven for refugees, when he had to flee Saxony with a price on his head, after his participation in the Dresden revolution in 1849.

It is harder to place the other hill, the Venusberg. (Some enterprising travel office might make a fortune on a theme park there, should they find it.) Thuringia is dotted with hills, however, and only a few miles from the Wartburg is an eminence called the Hörselberg (possibly, 'the hill where you can hear souls'). The Brothers Grimm have preserved another tale about this hill in which 'the devil lives and to which the witches make pilgrimages. Sometimes fearful shrieks and howls come from it.' The Brothers tell how, in the fourteenth century, fires broke out near Eisenach, joined together in one great mass of flame, and swept towards the Hörselberg. And when the townsfolk followed the fire they could see and hear, inside the hill, souls burning in hellfire.[6] Once again, the identification was too good *not* to use.

So, as in all ten of his major operas, Wagner shaped a mass of historical and legendary material into a workable three-act story and projected it onto a landscape that would express that story symbolically: all the scenes in *Tannhäuser* take place either within the pagan Venusberg or within the confronting Christian Wartburg, or deep in the valley between them.

I'm going to tell what happens in the three acts of Wagner's opera, and – as this is a story some of you already know all too well – I shall try to add details along the way that may be new to you, or may at least enable you to see the familiar plot in new ways.

The overture, a concert-hall favourite, leaves no doubt that through the opera there will rage a battle between sacred and profane, between the saintly and the sensual, between the pious chant of the German pilgrims on their way to seek forgiveness in Rome and the seductive strains of the votaries of Venus in her underworld grotto. But there is also an indication in the overture, something affirmed at the end of the opera, that this work will not be a celebration of the victory of sacred *over* profane, or of Christianity over paganism, or of Wartburg over Venusberg. It will be an acknowledgment of the importance of *both* worlds, an integration, even a synthesis, of the two worlds. At the end of the overture (in the early, Dresden version) the pilgrim's chorus is repeated, wreathed around with the pulsing music of Venus. Sacred and profane are reconciled. All of Wagner's operas synthesize, integrate, and make whole: what he could not do in his life he did in his art.

When, after the overture, the curtains part, we see an

elaborate depiction, amid mists, shafts of light, and cascading fountains, of the endless rituals of Venus – celebrated by mythic naiads, sirens, graces, nymphs, maenads, bacchants, satyrs, and fauns. According to the romances of the Middle Ages, the gods and spirits of pagan antiquity did not die: they only passed beneath the earth; they are still waiting to reveal themselves to any mortal who will seek them out. This is a tradition that Schiller, Hölderlin, and other German Romantics drew on.

Yet amid the rosy pagan mists Tannhäuser is dreaming of his green Germany, a place where trees still blossom and men still pray. He wakes in Venus's arms to what seems to be the sound of a distant church bell. How long, he asks, has it been since he has seen the sky, felt the sun, heard the nightingale? Venus bids him take his lyre and sing of her, but with each repetition of his song he forgets his erotic theme and longs for a normal life: 'In the midst of pleasure I long for pain. I want the freedom to struggle and to strive, even if it means my destruction and my death.'

Venus is furious, and threatens, if he leaves her, to withdraw venereal pleasure from all the earth; he will be cursed and rejected on his return there. 'You'll come back to me in the end,' she says, 'to seek salvation.'

'Salvation!' exclaims Tannhäuser. 'My salvation lies in Mary!' At this mention of the blessed Virgin, Venus and all her realm disappear, and we see green trees, clear sky, a roadside shrine to the Virgin, and, piping on a hill to the accompaniment of sheep-bells, an innocent shepherd boy. We are in the valley between the Venusberg and the

Wartburg, both hills looming visibly in the background. And Tannhäuser is suddenly there, astonished, kneeling before the statue of the Virgin on the very spot, it seems, where he had knelt before Venus. A band of pilgrims approaches the shrine, on their way to Rome. They sing the praises of Mary, the 'Jungfrau süss und rein,' and the shepherd boy calls after them, 'Glück auf nach Röm! Pray there for my poor soul.' Suddenly the penitent Tannhäuser breaks the stillness with a radiant high G that, sung by that great tenor Lauritz Melchior, year after year, for a full twelve Met broadcasts, was always a *coup de théâtre*. 'Praise to thee, almighty God,' Tannhäuser sings, 'for the miracles of thy grace are very great!'

The valley fills to the sound of hunting horns. Landgraf Hermann and his knightly minnesingers appear, and recognize Tannhäuser – because years before he had sung in the contests with them, and then had left them arrogantly. Does he come now as friend or foe? The gentlest of the knights, Wolfram, offers his hand to the erring knight. 'Stay with us, for Elisabeth's sake,' he sings, to one of the loveliest tunes in the whole operatic canon, an almost Italianate aria. (You may remember at this point that a near-starving Wagner had once put bread on his table by making instrumental arrangements of pieces by that accomplished Italian melodist, Gaetano Donizetti.)

The gentle Wolfram sings how there used to be something in Tannhäuser's music – call it magic or the purity of his art – that deeply affected Elisabeth, and that when he left their circle she never came to the singing contests again. In a moment, all the minstrel knights are pleading in the same melodious strain for Tannhäuser to come back to them. He is touched, this renegade from their society. He stays.

We've met our alienated hero. Now we are ready for what Goethe called the eternal feminine, the 'Ewig-Weibliche.' In Act II we're up inside the Wartburg, in the great central hall where the song contests are held – that room you can still visit today. Elisabeth bursts open its doors and greets the hall of song, which she has not seen since Tannhäuser's departure. She sings what has become *the* aria with which to open festivities in opera houses around the world: 'Dich, teure Halle' – 'Thee, beloved hall.'

In that hall of song, Wolfram brings Tannhäuser to the chaste Elisabeth, and quietly leaves them alone together. It is a time for confessions and admissions, but they are both hesitant. She asks, 'Where have you been so long away?' He only answers, 'Far, far from here. The one thing I remember now is that I never thought I would see you again.'

She says, 'Help me to understand what troubles my heart. Here in the hall of song I used to listen to the other singers with pleasure, but *your* songs awakened a whole new world within me: they would thrill me with pain, and pierce me with joy. I felt emotions I had never felt before, longings I had never known.' He says, and it is significant, that it was the god of love who touched his lyre and spoke to her in those songs.

The fatherly Landgraf enters the hall to take Elisabeth in his arms and tell her that the guests for the singing that day have come from far and near, for they have heard that, after a long absence, *she* will be the lady honoured by the song contest once again. And to some very familiar fanfares the hall fills with knights, ladies, page boys, and the six contesting minnesingers, with their minstrel lyres. The Landgraf announces that the theme for their songs this day will be 'What is love?', and that the winner of the contest will be crowned by Elisabeth, and may seek her hand. She draws from an urn the name of the first contestant, and the page boys formally announce it: 'Wolfram von Eschenbach, beginne.'

The virtuous Wolfram sings of courtly love, of a fountain full of grace; it quickens his heart, but never, never would he touch it; it is his duty to suffer and sacrifice himself for it, even to his last drop of blood. And that, he says, is what love is.

In the early Dresden version of the opera, Walther von der Vogelweide sings next, and goes even further in this chaste, knightly direction. Then, in both the Dresden and Paris versions, Tannhäuser rises unbidden from his place. The singers, he says, have completely misrepresented love. The art they have devoted themselves to – courtly, sacred love – is an illusion, a perversion. *God* and his stars cannot be reached, and so one praises *them* from afar. But human love – that is something that presses one to flesh like one's own. He lifts his lyre to sing the very song he sang to Venus in the Venusberg, all but admitting that, since his disappearance from their midst, he has been there. The shocked women flee the hall, and the men surround him with their drawn swords. Elisabeth, with a high B-natural that Kirsten Flagstad made wonderfully effective, throws herself between Tannhäuser and his attackers. (Flagstad only sang the role four times on the broadcasts; she had to share Melchior on the air with Maria Jeritza, Elisabeth Rethberg, Lotte Lehmann, Maria Müller, Astrid Varnay, and Helen Traubel. Those were great Wagner years at the Met.)

The impetuous Tannhäuser repents of his singing the praises of carnal love, not because he has offended the sensibilities of the Wartburg, but because he has brought suffering – and disgrace in the eyes of her subjects – to Elisabeth. The Landgraf suggests that he join the pilgrims still leaving Germany during the present holy year, when plenary indulgences are available to penitents travelling to Rome. The knights, less clement, say that if Tannhäuser *doesn't* seek pardon, they will kill him. From the valley below, we hear the pilgrims chanting on their way to Rome. Tannhäuser, not for the others in the Wartburg but for Elisabeth alone, rushes off, after kissing the hem of her garment, to join the penitents.

In Act III, we are back in the valley between the two confronting hills – only now the valley is not green with spring, but cheerless in faded autumn colours. Elisabeth is kneeling amid falling leaves before the shrine of the Virgin. Wolfram is standing at a distance. We hear the song of the pilgrims returning from Rome. They pass through the valley, singing how their penitence has brought them pardon. Elisabeth rises and anxiously scans their faces. Tannhäuser is not among them. 'He is not coming back,' she sings. She falls one last time on her knees before the Virgin, and asks her to take her life in return for Tannhäuser's salvation. Then, in a long word-

less scene which requires delicate acting (there is one of
these in every Wagner opera), she takes the path upwards to the castle and is lost from view.

Night comes on. Wolfram looks up and sees the sky
pierced by the evening star. He lifts his lyre and asks the
star to greet Elisabeth's soul as it passes from earth to
heaven. The song, a very beautiful one, marks the
moment when Elisabeth, above in the Wartburg, dies.

Then comes the greatest scene in the opera. A solitary
figure appears in the darkness. 'I heard the sound of a
minstrel's lyre,' it says in strange, almost sardonic tones.
'How sad it seemed.' Wolfram hardly recognizes Tannhäuser, a shadowy, forbidding figure who will not let
himself be touched. 'Zurück von mir' ('Keep away from
me'), he cries. 'The place where I rest is accursed.' Melchior was heartbreaking at that moment.

Tannhäuser tells the stunned Wolfram how he made
his pilgrimage to Rome in a true spirit of penitence:
when the others trod on the meadows, he sought thorns
and stones for his bare feet; when others drank of the
cool springs, he drank in the sun's scorching heat; when,
crossing the Alps, the others sheltered in a hospice, he
slept amid snow and ice; when they descended from the
mountains to Italy's beautiful valleys, he, in penance,
went blindfolded so as not to see the loveliness of the
land.

'And then,' he sings, 'I came to Rome. All the bells
were ringing. Hymns were floating down from the vault
of the great church. A cry of joy burst from the crowd,
that grace and healing would be given to us all. Then I
saw him through whom God speaks. All the people knelt

before him. And thousands he gave grace to. He par-
doned them by thousands and told them to rise. But
when I drew near and confessed my sins, the terrible lust
my senses had experienced, the desires that no penances
had stilled, when I cried out to him to save me – he to
whom I prayed replied:
"If you have felt such evil lust
As in the flames of hell is nursed,
If in the Venusberg you've dwelt,
You are forevermore accursed.
And, as this staff within my hand
Ne'er will put forth a living leaf,
So from the burning fires of hell
Never will you find relief."
I sank down in despair. My senses left me. When at last I
came to, it was dark, and the square was deserted. Far
away I could hear the happy songs of grace. They sick-
ened me, those holy songs!'
   Wolfram has listened in horror and pity. 'Now,' Tannhäuser says, 'I shall return to the Venusberg.' That
mountain in the distance begins to glow with rosy light.
Mists emanate from it towards the valley. Voluptuous
music fills the air. Venus appears in the distance and
sings, 'Did the world cast you out? Come to me. The
fountain of love flows here forever.' Wolfram tries to
hold his friend back, and (the parallels with Act i are, as
so often in Wagner, coming clear) Wolfram sings, once
again, 'Elisabeth.' The rosy mists are pierced by the glow
of candles from the Wartburg. It is Elisabeth's funeral
cortege approaching. Venus and her mists disappear.
Tannhäuser sinks on Elisabeth's body, dying himself,

singing, with the words of the Litany of Saints, 'Saint Elisabeth, pray for me.'

Suddenly another group of pilgrims enters – innocent boys returning from Rome and bearing the pope's staff, which has blossomed in green leaves.

Wagner went on to compose more profound and disturbing dramas than *Tannhäuser*, and this early work that was once thought outrageously chromatic, the eye of a musical storm if not the end of music itself, now seems to some little more than a collection of too-familiar tunes, and a simplistic conflict between good and evil – indeed an unconvincing victory of good *over* evil. And at the end of this troubled century, when we are not so sure as we once were about the moral standards and structures that once sustained us, we reject moralizing oversimplifications, perhaps especially when they come in dramatic form. *Tannhäuser*, at the turn of the twentieth century one of the three or four most popular operas in the world, is not nearly so popular today, far outdistanced in popularity by Wagner's mature works, not to mention those of Mozart, Verdi, Puccini, and Richard Strauss.

But is *Tannhäuser* simplistic? It is set in a historical era of some complexity – at a time when a stable, nominally Christian society, confident of its artistic, political, and spiritual values, was challenged by a renascent paganism, a new spirit that was drawing to itself the most creative elements in Christendom. It will help us to appreciate *Tannhäuser* if we see its hero as a man torn, not between good and evil, but between two opposing sets of values, each important and essential to him. Landgraf

Hermann in his cliffed, commanding Wartburg, the minnesingers with their chaste and courtly approach to the
problems of human existence, the Thuringian knights
with their sword-wielding moralizing – these represent
the Middle Ages. Venus, with her open sensuality and
her mythological following – naiads, nymphs, satyrs, and
fauns – is an evocation of the Renaissance. The visions at
her court – Leda and the swan, Europa and the bull, the
three Graces linked arm in arm – are Renaissance pic-
tures. The values that Tannhäuser draws from his experience in the Venusberg and expresses in his songs in the
Wartburg are neo-pagan: one should put his hands and
his lips to all that is lovable and not idealize it from afar.
The cultural climate is changing, and Tannhäuser is the
first to sense it. Small wonder the knights in the Wartburg
draw their swords, and Urban IV in Rome withholds his
absolution. The new paganism threatens the very foun-
dations of the civilization they know.

The movement from medieval to Renaissance is one of
the great moments in Western history and in Western
consciousness, and it was not effected without a struggle
and a synthesis. The significance of *Tannhäuser* is that in
it Wagner has caught the tension of that historic moment
and centred it in the soul of his hero. His Tannhäuser is a
man torn between two worlds, unable to rest in either.
Cursed with insatiability by his pagan goddess, damned
for eternity by his Christian pontiff, he struggles to
understand himself after his soul has been wrenched
apart. His only hope is to rise above his two experiences
and achieve a new synthesis of them – a synthesis the
Western world strove for more than a century to achieve.

But *Tannhäuser* is still more than that. If we look past
the period in which it is set, to the time when it was composed, we can place it at another important moment in
cultural history. Nineteenth-century German Romantic
poets, looking for a kind of renaissance in *their* day, sang
that the gods of pagan antiquity had never died but only
passed beneath the earth, where they were still waiting
to reveal themselves to any mortal who would seek them
out and believe in them. 'Schöne Welt, wo bist du?' was
Schiller's question, set to music by Schubert: 'Beautiful
world, where are you?' The Romantic German looked to
both the spirit of classical Greece and to his own medieval past, his own forests and song-birds, for his inspiration. Goethe, Winckelmann, Heine, and, early in our own
century, Stefan George and Gerhart Hauptmann – all in
their several ways dealt with the conflict of Christian and
neo-Hellenic paganism in the artist's soul. Hölderin, in
'Sonnenuntergang' and other classic poems, saw Romantic Germany awakening the gods of Greece from their
centuries of slumber. Gottfried Keller in his childlike but
seriously intended story 'Das Tanzlegendschen' showed
the Virgin Mary interceding for the admission of the nine
pagan Muses into the presence of the Trinity.

Wagner's questing Tannhäuser is that sort of Romantic
– the pagan Christian seeking to know himself. He is like
that essential German mythic figure, Faust. (It is an inter-
esting coincidence that both Goethe's hero and Wagner's
are called Heinrich by the women who save them.) Like
Faust, Tannhäuser is a creative artist in whom two souls
dwell, a man who must search and strive, and err so long
as he strives, and win what Wagner called 'redemption'

at the moment of death through the intercession of an 'Ewig-Weibliche,' a saving, eternal feminine. That last line of Goethe's *Faust* – 'the eternal feminine leads us upward' – is the very essence of German Romanticism. Man may strive (through art and reason and physical force) towards a synthesis of human experience, but it is woman who (through intuition, tenderness, and a different kind of courage) points the way to achieving it.

Wagner often quoted Goethe's last line about 'the eternal feminine' saving a man, and Robert Donington, in his Jungian analysis of the *Ring*, says rightly, 'If we cannot understand this final theme of redemption, we cannot understand Wagner. It was his lifelong preoccupation.'[7] Who more than Wagner needed 'redeeming' from himself? Who more than Wagner saw the possibility of that redemption in what psychiatrists today call 'the feminine principle' in himself? Wagner was in fact writing an essay on the importance of the feminine principle within a man the day he died.

Elisabeth, then, is more important in this opera than we may at first have thought. It is often said that Elisabeth serves as a foil for Venus in the opera. But surely the Virgin Mary is the figure set against Venus – the sacred set against the profane, the medieval against the Renaissance. Elisabeth is a central character, as central as Tannhäuser himself, leading the way for him. She comes to know something of both of his worlds. Steadfast in her Christian faith, she also feels the stirring of the new paganism. She confesses that Tannhäuser's songs brought to her 'a strange new life ... emotions I had never felt before, longings I had never known.' Wolfram speaks of Tannhäuser's songs as having cast some kind of spell over her. Elisabeth even admits, in her prayer to the Virgin, that she has had to struggle with the new, disturbing feelings she has felt in Tannhäuser's music.

It is Elisabeth who achieves first what the tormented Tannhäuser is searching for. In Act III she asks the Virgin to take her life and then, without a word, ascends to the Wartburg to die. Like so many deaths in Wagner, Elisabeth's comes of no natural cause, and must be taken symbolically. She has the mission of the saving woman who, at the end of Goethe's *Faust*, kneels at the feet of the Virgin Mary and leads the hero's striving soul upwards, where the struggling elements within him are reconciled.

Wagner's opera ends with two deaths and two symbols. First, Elisabeth dies, and the evening twilight is pierced by a star – appropriately enough, as Elisabeth has been likened to a star throughout the opera. I think, however, that the evening star in *Tannhäuser* can mean something more than is usually made of it. (Wagner's intuition at the close of his operas invariably surfaces in his most expressive symbols.) What we call the evening star is an ambivalent symbol: it is both the planet Venus and, in the morning, she whom medieval Christians called the 'stella matutina,' the Virgin Mary, the morning star. In Donington's terms the star, with its two opposed associations, is a symbol of psychic wholeness, and its appearance at the moment of Elisabeth's death an indication that she has, with feminine insight, reconciled the two worlds her beloved still struggles with. Now she will light the way for him.

Then Tannhäuser dies, again of no physical causes,

and new pilgrims arrive from Rome carrying the Pope's staff, blossoming with green leaves. The symbolism here is Christian, from Wagner's medieval sources, but we should not limit its application to Christianity. In fact, Wagner dismissed 'those critics who would read into my *Tannhäuser* a specifically Christian meaning, and a weak, pietistic one at that.'[8] What we have, again, is a sign that opposing values have been reconciled. The greening of the papal sceptre will suggest to Jungians like Donington the healing of the hero's psyche after it has been torn apart by conflicting experiences; for Wagner's terms 'grace,' 'redemption,' and 'salvation,' they will read psychological healing, wholeness, and transformation. It is equally possible to see the blossoming sceptre as a symbol of two eras and two ideals: in it medieval Christendom has accepted the values of Renaissance paganism.

But ultimately in Wagner it is the music that must explain the symbol, and Wagner does not disappoint us here: just as the papal staff has sprouted leaves, so, as the opera ends, Wagner's Christian hymn, the famous 'Pilgrim's Chorus,' is surrounded by an instrumental figure from the pulsing music of Wagner's Venusberg. As Wagner himself explained, apropos of the overture where we heard the first hint of this, 'With the hymn of God we hear the joyous sound of the Venusberg, no longer profane but redeemed ... pulsing, welling up, leaping; the two forces, the spiritual and the sensual, once separated, now embrace.'[9]

Tannhäuser is not, then, a dramatization of the victory of sacred over profane, of spirit over flesh, of Christianity over paganism. It is a celebration of a synthesis of those opposites, the healing of a soul torn between two worlds. Who are we reminded of in all of this? Well, so long as we are in Germany at the beginnings of a new era, Tannhäuser should remind us of another tormented young protester who was gifted in song, clashed with the Pope, sought refuge in the Wartburg, defied the society he knew, and profoundly changed it. Did Wagner have Martin Luther in mind as he wrote?[10]

Or is Wagner's hero a projection of himself? The composer of *Tannhäuser* was, like his hero, soon to stop at the Wartburg on his way to political exile with a price on his head. He was soon to act out his own scenario – scorned and attacked for his revolutionary music, shocking the bourgeoisie with his scandalous sex life, driven by the demon in him to write even more fervid dramas of neo-pagan redemption, a musician unable to win a hearing because of his unorthodoxy, an adventurer who insisted that sexuality be experienced and not idealized, a social outcast who had reached a state of awareness beyond that of his contemporaries. In the context of nineteenth-century music, Schumann and Brahms, like the minne-singers at the Wartburg, could not understand him. Only Liszt, a trusty Wolfram, would take his part. But what did that Wolfram know of the fires that consumed him? Fortunately, there would be a number of Elisabeths to help him through his spiritual crises. In short, Wagner was the Tannhäuser of his time.

But, to return to the main concern of these lectures, let me say again that, even in a work of art that is to some extent auto- or psycho-biographical, 'it is [the] art that

explains the artist, and not the insufficiencies and conflicts of his personal life.' That is a quotation from Carl
Jung, who goes on to say, as we said when we first spoke
about the *Philoctetes* of Sophocles here, 'The lives of artists are as a rule unsatisfactory – not to say tragic –
because of their inferiority on the human and personal
side ... There is hardly any exception to the rule that a
person must pay dearly for the divine gift of creative
fire.'[11] The products of creative fire have meaning for any
of us who is human, but Jung warns us: 'We completely
miss [that] meaning if we try to derive it from personal
factors,' from the unedifying life of the creative artist,
from the shallows of his personal views ... Great art
'draws its strength from the life of mankind.'[12] Ultimately the self-absorbed Wagner wrote for the rest of us.

   Tannhäuser speaks for all of us. I said at first that it was
a young man's opera. For a production in Houston a
generation ago I wrote a piece about its hero being a figure for the troubled drop-out Romantics of the sixties –
youths openly protesting, at odds with themselves and
with society, obsessed with sex, flaunting their psyche-
delic experiences in violent new musical styles. But that
era is long since gone, and *Tannhäuser*, like any true classic, continues to speak. Its hero is anyone who reaches a
level of awareness that makes it impossible for him, or
her, to return to older, simpler, more innocent ways. It
speaks for anyone who has ever had to relate a whole
new world of intellectual or spiritual or sensual revela-
tions to the older, traditional values of the world in
which he is placed. I imagine that most of us who love
music or art or literature or philosophy have had, at

some time in our lives, to struggle through that sort of crisis. Perhaps we came through it only with the help of someone who loved us and led us upward out of our despair. *Tannhäuser* shows us a soul undergoing that experience, struggling to know itself. When the tormented Baudelaire first heard *Tannhäuser* he wrote humbly to Wagner to say, 'Thank you ... you have brought me back in touch with myself.'[13]

Most of us will at sometime or other have been spoken to, and perhaps even sustained by, some great work of art. I have always believed that great works of art are not just gifts from God to His artists, like the bow was to Philoctetes, but God's testaments to all humankind, testaments through which He speaks, even though the interpretation of works of art can be as problematic as is the interpretation of the scriptural testaments. God speaks to us through works of art. In a famous poem by Rainer Maria Rilke a centuries-old torso of Apollo, gleaming like a star at the places where the head, the limbs, and the genitals have been broken off, looks back at Rilke (though of course the torso has no eyes), speaks to him (though of course the torso has no mouth), and says – the god says – 'Du musst dein Leben ändern' – 'You must change your life.'

Thomas Mann, recounting in his story 'Schwere Stunde' the 'difficult hour' through which the young Schiller struggled to complete a poem, affirmed, in biblical language, that the finished work contained, not just the artist's humanity, but something of the divinity that the artist was privileged to know:

And it was finished, that labour of suffering ... And when

it was finished, behold, it was good. And then out of his soul, out of music and idea, new works struggled forth, ringing and gleaming structures, which in sacred form wondrously granted a vision of the infinite source from which they came – just as, in the shell that has been fished out of the sea, the roar of the sea can still be heard.

God speaks to us through works of art. What is it that we have a right to expect great art to say to us, to do for us? To delight us, of course, but also to deepen our awareness of the things that matter, to enable us to accept darkness and pain, to tell us what we might not have wanted to know but needed to know, to make us into something more than we were before, more human and more compassionate. And, most of all I think, to enable us to see into ourselves.[14] Bernard Shaw, in his most Wagnerian play, *Back to Methuselah*, said, 'You use a glass mirror to see your face: you use works of art to see your soul.'

Tannhäuser is the work that first enabled me to do that, in 1942. It is a youthful work, and it speaks to the young, but it is also, like all art worthy of the name, a work that can speak to you at any time in your life. It was of special importance to Wagner, not just in his late twenties but through all his seventy years: the week he died he declared his intention to return to it and give it the musical consistency it had never, with conflicting Dresden and Paris versions, enjoyed. It spoke for him, for his wounded self, for the demons that drove him from within, for the conflicting emotions that tore him apart, for the integration he never achieved in his life but sang of eloquently – and eventually achieved – in his art.

So, no less than the greater works that followed it, *Tannhäuser* tells us something of why a man perceived as a terrible man can produce beautiful and ultimately healing works of art. That is the issue I have tried to address in these lectures. The intuitive Wagner saw deeper into human nature than the rest of us are likely to do. And so we need him, the wounded Philoctetes with the God-given power to see unerringly into ourselves and so to help us with our lives.

NOTES

1 Critics of Wagner often object, from a perfunctory reading of his *Opera and Drama* (1851), that he thought the text of an opera more important than the music. The thesis of Dahlhaus 1979 [1971], 156–7, generally accepted today, is that in Wagner's works neither music nor text is subordinate to, corresponds to, supports, or illustrates the other. What they do is interact, in highly complex ways. And each is only a means of expression used to realize the overall dramatic concept. The dramatic achievements of Sophocles and Shakespeare, of Molière and Mozart – none of whom figures in Dahlhaus's difficult but illuminating book – are surely of a stature comparable to Wagner's, but are produced by less intricately expressive means.

2 In Lee 1995, 81–9. Some of that material is reproduced here.

3 From 'Tannhäuser,' Hanslick's very first review for the *Wiener Musikzeitung*, November 1846. In Hanslick 1950, 35–6.

4 Letter of 17 February 1860. Quoted in Barth, Mack, and Voss 1975, 193.

5 From 'A Communication to My Friends' (1851). Wagner 1911–16, vol. 4, 279. As the only English translation of this and other prose works of Wagner is now badly dated, the translation here is my own.

6 Recorded in Newman 1949, 72. Newman, still a valuable reference

for many of Wagner's *Tannhäuser* sources, may now be supple-
mented by Spencer 1988, 17–24.

7 Donington 1974 [1963], 260.

8 From 'A Communication to My Friends' (1851). Wagner 1911–16,
   vol. 4, 279. The translation is my own.

9 From 'The Overture to *Tannhäuser*' (1852). Wagner 1911–16, vol. 5,
   178–9. The translation is my own. It might be objected that the
   'pulsing music' of paganism also appears in combination with the
   Christian hymn not just at the opera's end but earlier in Act III,
   when the pilgrims return from Rome without Tannhäuser, and
   when there seems no possibility at all of any reconciliation of his
   pagan and Christian experiences. There is no easy answer to this
   objection. Perhaps we are to think that, when those first pilgrims
   arrive back in Thuringia, the pope's staff has, unbeknownst to
   them, already blossomed (the second band of pilgrims appears
   with it within the hour). But that is a kind of dramatic irony more
   appropriate to the later Wagner. I rather suspect that this is one of
   the passages Wagner had in mind when, in later life and even a
   few days before his death, he spoke to Cosima about making
   changes in *Tannhäuser* to give it the consistency it had always
   lacked. See *Cosima Wagner's Diaries* 1977, entries for 19 October
   1881, 6 October 1882; and 23 January and 6 February 1883.

10 In 1868, to mark the 350th anniversary of the Reformation, Wagner began a prose sketch called *Luthers Hochzeit*, on the reformer's
   renunciation of Catholicism and his marriage to a former nun.
   Wagner's uncompleted Luther project to some extent paralleled
   his experience at the time: he was cohabiting with Cosima, but not
   able to marry her for another two years, and meanwhile, to facili-
   tate her divorce from Hans von Bülow, he wanted her to renounce
   her Catholic faith, which she did in 1872. According to Newman
   1976, vol. 4, 160, 'The sketch shows Luther very much as Wagner
   saw himself just then – looking out from the Wartburg upon the
   beautiful world outside his window, troubled with himself,
   doubtful of himself and all things, but strengthened in his soul by
   the glance of a woman's eye and the glint of her golden hair.' All
   of this was more than twenty years after the premiere of *Tann-*

häuser, but then ten years later still Wagner was considering work on the Luther project again, and (see note 4) in the weeks before he died he was still speaking of giving *Tannhäuser* its final form. His life seemed almost invariably to pervade his works of art.

11 Jung 1955, 195–6.
12 Ibid., 191.
13 Letter of 17 February 1860. Quoted in Barth, Mack, and Voss 1975, 193.
14 Remarks paraphrased from the 1990 PBS telecast 'Bill Moyers in Conversation with Sister Wendy,' with gratitude.

BIBLIOGRAPHY

This bibliography includes only those works consulted or cited in the notes, and is in no way intended as a list of the most important works on Wagner.

Barth, Herbert, Dietrich Mack, and Egon Voss. 1975. *Wagner: A Documentary Study.* Translated by P.R.J. Ford and Mary Whittall. London: Thames and Hudson.

Beckett, Lucy. 1979. 'Wagner and His Critics.' In Burbidge and Sutton 1979, 365–88.

– 1981. *Parsifal.* Cambridge: Cambridge University Press.

Bernstein, Leonard. 1991 [1985]. 'Wagner's music isn't racist.' *New York Times.* Op-Ed page, Thursday, 26 December.

Blissett, William. 1959. 'Ernest Newman and English Wagnerism.' *Music and Letters* 40: 311–23.

– 1960. 'Thomas Mann: The Last Wagnerite.' *Germanic Review* 35: 50–76.

_ 1961. 'George Moore and Literary Wagnerism.' *Comparative Literature* 13: 52–71.

– 1963. 'Wagnerian Fiction in English.' *Criticism* 5: 239–60.

– 1966a. 'Stephan Dedalus in the Smithy of His Soul.' In Thomas F. Staley, ed., *James Joyce Today.* Bloomington: Indiana University Press.

– 1966b. 'D.H. Lawrence, D'Annunzio, Wagner.' *Contemporary Literature*, 21–46.

– 1978. 'Wagner in *The Waste Land.*' In *The Practical Vision: Essays in English Literature in Honour of Flora Roy,* 71–85. Waterloo, Ont.: Waterloo University Press.

Borchmeier, Dieter. 1992 [1986]. 'The Question of Anti-Semitism.' Translated by Stewart Spencer. In Müller and Wapnewski 1992, 166–85.

96   Bibliography

Burbidge, Peter, and Richard Sutton. 1979. *The Wagner Companion.* New York: Cambridge University Press.

Cairns, David. 1973. *Responses: Musical Essays and Reviews.* New York: Alfred A Knopf.

Carabine, Keith. 1984. 'Introduction' to Joseph Conrad, *Nostromo: A Tale of the Seaboard.* Oxford: Oxford University Press.

Cornwell, John. 1997. 'A genius on the couch.' *The Tablet*, 25 January 1997: 104–5.

Dahlhaus, Carl. 1979 [1971]. *Richard Wagner's Music Dramas.* Translated by Mary Whittall. New York: Cambridge University Press.

Deathridge, John, and Carl Dahlhaus. 1984. *The New Grove Wagner.* New York: W.W. Norton.

Donington, Robert. 1974 [1963]. *Wagner's 'Ring' and Its Symbols.* London: Faber and Faber.

– 1976. 'Wagner and *Die Meistersinger.*' *Opera News*, 17 April 1976: 18–19.

Dubal, David. 1984. *Reflections from the Keyboard.* New York: Summit Books.

Furness, Raymond. 1992. 'Wagner's Impact on Literature.' In Millington 1992, 396–8.

Gilson, Étienne. 1953. *Choir of the Muses.* Translated by Maisie Ward. New York: Sheed and Ward.

Gregor-Dellin, Martin. 1983 [1980]. *Richard Wagner: His Life. His Work. His Century.* Translated by J. Maxwell Brownjohn. New York: Harcourt Brace Jovanovich.

Hall, Michael. 1992. 'Wagner's Impact on the Visual Arts.' In Millington 1992, 398–401.

Hanslick, Eduard. 1950 [1848–99]. *Music Criticisms.* Translated by Henry Pleasants. Harmondsworth: Penguin Books.

Holloway, Robin. 1979. 'Tristan und Isolde.' In Alan Blyth, ed., *Opera on Record.* London: Hutchison and Co.

Horowitz, Joseph. 1978. 'He has made peace with Romanticism.' *New York Times*, 10 December.

– 1998. 'Nothing approaching caricature.' *Times Literary Supplement*, 21 August: 16–17.

Jackson Knight, W.F. 1936. *Cumaean Gates*. Oxford: Basil Blackwell.
John, Nicholas, editor. 1988. *Tannhäuser*. New York: Riverrun Press.
Jung, C.J. 1955 [1933]. *Modern Man in Search of a Soul*. New York: Harcourt, Brace.
Kühnel, Jürgen. 1992. 'The Prose Writings.' In Müller and Wapnewski 1992, 565–651.
Large, David C. 1992. 'The Bayreuth Legacy.' In Millington 1992, 389–92.
Large, David C., and William Weber, editors. 1984. *Wagnerism in European Culture and Politics*. Ithaca: Cornell University Press.
Lee, M. Owen. 1990. *Wagner's Ring: Turning the Sky Round*. New York: Summit Books.
– 1995. *First Intermissions*. New York: Oxford University Press.
– 1998. *A Season of Opera: From Orpheus to Ariadne*. Toronto: University of Toronto Press.
Levin, Bernard. ca. 1993. 'Music from the depths.' *London Times*.
Magee, Bryan. 1988 [1968]. *Aspects of Wagner*. Oxford: Oxford University Press.
Marek, George R. 1957. *The World Treasury of Grand Opera*. New York: Harper and Brothers.
Mann, Thomas. 1933. 'Sufferings and Greatness of Richard Wagner.' Translated by H.T. Lowe-Porter. In Marek 1957, 316–62.
May, Rollo. 1975. *The Courage to Create*. New York: W.W. Norton.
Millington, Barry, editor. 1992. *The Wagner Compendium*. New York: Schirmer Books.
Müller, Ulrich, and Peter Wapnewski. 1992. *Wagner Handbook*. Edited by John Deathridge. Cambridge, Mass.: Harvard University Press.
Newman, Ernest. 1949. *Wagner Nights*. London: Putnam & Company. Reprinted as *The Wagner Operas*. Princeton, NJ: Princeton University Press, 1991.
– 1976 [1937–47]. *The Life of Richard Wagner*. 4 volumes. Cambridge: Cambridge University Press.
Rather, L.J. 1990. *Reading Wagner: A Study in the History of Ideas*. Baton Rouge: Louisiana State University Press.
Rougement, Denis de. 1974 [1939]. *Love in the Western World*. Translated by Montgomery Belgion. New York: Harper and Row.

Sabor, Rudolph. *The Real Wagner*. 1987. London: André Deutsch.

Spencer, Stewart. 1988. 'Tanhusaere, Danheüser and Tannhäuser.' In John 1988, 17–24.

Spencer, Stewart, and Barry Millington, editors. 1987. *Selected Letters of Richard Wagner*. New York: W.W. Norton.

Swanston, Hamish F.G. 1978. *In Defense of Opera*. Harmondsworth: Penguin Books.

Tanner, Michael. 1979. 'The Total Work of Art.' In Burbidge and Sutton, 1979, 140–224.

Taylor, Deems. 1937. 'The Monster.' In *Of Men and Music*. Reprinted in Marek 1957, 363–6.

Vaget, Hans Rudolf. 1993. 'Wagner, Anti-Semitism, and Mr. Rose: *Merkwürd'ger Fall.*' *German Quarterly* 66(2): 222–36.

Vetter, Isolde. 1992. 'Wagner in the History of Psychology.' Translated by Stewart Spencer. In Müller and Wapnewski 1992, 118–55.

Wagner, Cosima. 1977 [1878–83]. *Cosima Wagner's Diaries*. Translated by Geoffrey Skelton. 2 volumes. New York: Harcourt Brace Jovanovich.

Wagner, Richard. 1911–16. *Sämtliche Schriften und Dichtungen (Volksausgabe)*. 12 volumes. Leipzig: Breitkopf and Härtel.

– 1980 [1865–82]. *The Brown Book*. Translated by George Bird. London: Cambridge University Press.

Walker, Alan. 1997. 'Wagner: A problem without a solution.' *Globe and Mail* (Toronto) 1 March 1997, 17.

Weiner, Marc A. 1980. 'Zwieback and Madeleine: Creative Recall in Wagner and Proust.' *MLN* 95: 679–84.

Westernhagen, Curt von. 1981 [1977]. *Wagner: A Biography*. Translated by Mary Whittall. Cambridge: Cambridge University Press.

Whittall, Arnold. 1992. 'Wagner's Impact on the History of Music.' In Millington 1992, 393–96.

– 1996. 'Wagner and real life.' *The Musical Times*, June 1996: 5–11.

Wilson, Edmund. 1941. *The Wound and the Bow*. Cambridge, Mass.: Houghton Mifflin.

INDEX